AMAZING SPORTS FACTS

GEORGE SULLIVAN

SCHOLASTIC BOOK SERVICES
New York Toronto London Auckland Sydney Tokyo

Photo credits: George Sullivan: pp. 3, 9, 22, 28, 37, 47, 55, 86, 91, 103, 112, 118, 119, 141, 148, 173; Alf Ruelle: p. 65; National Baseball Library: p. 79; Rich Clarkson, Topeka Capital-Journal, Topeka, Kansas: p. 129; CBS-TV Sports: p. 189

ISBN: 0-590-12066-2

Published by Scholastic Book Services, a division of Scholastic Magazines, Inc.

12 11 10 9 8 7 6 5 1 2 3/8

Printed in the U.S.A. 01

Max Flack and Clifton Heathcote are the only men in major-league history to have played on two different teams in one day. How did it happen? On May 30, 1922, between games of a doubleheader in which Flack's club, the Chicago Cubs, faced Heathcote's team, the St. Louis Cardinals, one player was traded for the other.

During the 1975 bowling season, Steve Stevenson of Walla Walla, Washington, rolled 11 strikes in a row. One more and he'd have a 300 game — perfection. But just as Stevenson released his final ball, his foot edged over the foul line. The instant the foul buzzer sounded, Stevenson knew that he had blown his chance. His final score was 290.

The case of a bowler rolling 11 consecutive strikes and then not getting any pins at all on the 12th ball has occurred 13 times in bowling history. In seven instances the bowler has, like Stevenson, fouled on the 12th ball. In the other six cases, the 12th ball has been a gutter ball.

★ ★ ★

Martina Navratilova, a member of the Cleveland-Pittsburgh Nets of World Team Tennis, has what is believed to be the fastest serve in women's tennis. It has been clocked at 91 miles an hour.

★ ★ ★

There have been several instances of fathers and sons gaining prominence in professional football. But only once has a father-son combination earned entries in the National Football League record manual. On November 25, 1951, Bill (Dub) Jones, a running back for the Cleveland Browns, scored six touchdowns in a game against the Chicago Bears, tying a touchdown record that Ernie Nevers had established in 1929. On December 15, 1974, Bert Jones of the Baltimore Colts, Dub's son, completed a record 17 consecutive passes in a game against the New York Jets.

★ ★ ★

Only one triple play has occurred in World Series history, and that was unassisted. It occurred on October 10, 1920, in the fifth game of

Martina Navratilova

the Cleveland Indians/Brooklyn Dodgers series. Cleveland second baseman Bill Wambsganss caught Clarence Mitchell's line drive, stepped on second base to retire Pete Kilduff, and then tagged Otto Miller coming in from first. That isn't the only reason the game is historic. Half of Cleveland's runs in their 8-1 victory were driven in by Elmer Smith's grand-slam home run, the first grand slammer in World Series competition.

★ ★ ★

America's Marjorie Gestring became the youngest individual gold medal winner in Olympic history when she captured the springboard diving title at the Olympic Games in Berlin in 1936. Marjorie was 13 years old.

★ ★ ★

Individuals skilled in karate are able to split boards and bricks and wreak terrible damage with the sides of their hands. One of the most remarkable exhibitions in the destructive power of the karate "chop" was given at Bradford, England, several years ago. A team of 15 karate experts, using only their bare feet and hands, completely demolished a six-room, 150-year-old house. Once the house was reduced to a mass of rubble, the team faced the "defeated opponent" and bowed in the traditional manner.

★ ★ ★

When the Detroit Red Wings met the Montreal Maroons in a 1936 Stanley Cup hockey playoff game, the two teams battled through 60 minutes of play without either team scoring. Neither team scored in the first overtime period, and the game remained scoreless through the second, third, fourth, and fifth overtime periods. Finally, after 176 minutes and 30 seconds of play, Detroit's Modere (Mud) Bruneteau fired a searing 25-foot shot that beat Montreal goalie Lorne Chabot, ending the longest game in hockey history. Bruneteau had played only half a dozen games for Detroit, having spent most of the season with the Detroit Olympics of the International League, and the playoff game in which he fired the winning shot was the very first in which he participated.

★ ★ ★

Ty Cobb accumulated 4,191 hits during his major league baseball career, more than any other player. Cobb also holds the career record for singles (3,052) and the American League record for triples (297).

Cobb probably could have been one of baseball's leading home-run hitters, except that he played during baseball's "dead ball" era. As it was, he did lead the major leagues in home runs one year, in 1909, when he had nine of them. Yes, nine.

★ ★ ★

On February 13, 1975, Jerry Hill of Lawton, Oklahoma, bowled a 300 game. On August 4 that year, his wife, Norma, duplicated her husband's feat. This was not surprising to officials of the American Bowling Congress. There had been nine other instances of husbands and wives bowling perfect games. But then on October 24, 1976, the Hills' son Mark rolled a 300 game. That *was* surprising. Never before in bowling history had a father-mother-son combination achieved bowling perfection.

★ ★ ★

Bill Sharman, in his 11-year career with the Boston Celtics, established himself as one of the best foul shooters in the history of the National Basketball Association, if not *the* best. At the time of his retirement in 1961, Sharman owned the highest free-throw percentage of all time — .884 percent (3,143 free throws made on 3,557 attempts). During the 1958-59 season, Sharman made 342 of the 367 free throws he attempted, for a .932 percentage, the highest ever for a season. That same season, he made a record 56 consecutive free throws. (Calvin Murphy, with 58 straight free throws, set a new record during the 1975-76 season.)

Gene Conley, one of his teammates, once told of an index card that Sharman carried that listed things to remember during a game. "Every single night he read it," Conley said. "The card told him things like how to release the ball when shooting and how to position his feet when shooting. He was still reading the card at the end of his career."

Karen Yvette Muir became the youngest person in sports history to break a world record when, on August 10, 1965, she established a new mark for the women's 110-yard backstroke with a time of 1 minute, 8.7 seconds. The race was held at Blackpool, England. Karen was 12 years old at the time.

★ ★ ★

On May 18, 1912, when the Detroit Tigers visited Philadelphia to face the Athletics, Ty Cobb was not allowed to play, having been suspended for climbing into the stands to punish a heckler a few days before. "If Cobb doesn't play," said his teammates, "we won't play." Knowing that he would be fined $5,000 by the league if he did not field a team, Hugh Jennings, the manager of the Tigers, hired the baseball team from St. Joseph's College in Philadelphia for the day. It resulted in an embarrassing afternoon for the collegians, as they ended up losing, 24-2. All of the runs were charged to 20-year-old Aloysius Travers, establishing an all-time single-game record that still stands. His teammates contributed to Travers' downfall by committing nine errors.

Jennings also hired one sandlot player to fill in that afternoon. His name was Ed Irwin. He was the team's catcher. Irwin collected two hits, both triples, in the three times he came to bat, and in *The Official Encyclopedia of Baseball* he thus enjoys a lifetime batting average of .667.

★ ★ ★

The only sport in which competitors are not supposed to win, or accomplish what they have been trained to accomplish, is dog racing. The muzzled greyhounds pursue a mechanical "rabbit" that is mounted on a track and powered by electric current. Should one of the racers be successful in the chase and overtake his prey, the contest is immediately declared "no race."

★ ★ ★

In 1971, Billie Jean King became the first woman athlete to earn $100,000 in a year. During the same year, Rod Laver was the leading money winner in men's tennis. But because of the bigger amounts paid to male players, Billie Jean, to reach her total, had to win three times as many tournaments as Laver.

★ ★ ★

Some referees in the National Hockey League did not begin using whistles until the

Billie Jean King

1930's. Instead, they carried small bells that they tinkled at offenders.

★ ★ ★

When the Cincinnati Reds defeated the New York Yankees in the 1976 World Series, it was a tipoff that Jimmy Carter was going to beat Gerald Ford in the presidential election a few weeks later. It seems that there is a direct relationship between which league wins the World Series and which political party wins the ensuing presidential election. Ever since 1940, with only one exception (1948), when a National League team wins the World Series in an election year, the Democratic candidate captures the White House. When the American League wins, then so does a Republican. Here's an election-by-election rundown:

Year	*Series Winner*	*Election Winner*
1940	National League	Democrats (Franklin Roosevelt)
1944	National League	Democrats (Franklin Roosevelt)
1948	American League	Democrats (Harry Truman)
1952	American League	Republican (Dwight Eisenhower)
1956	American League	Republican (Dwight Eisenhower)
1960	National League	Democrats (John Kennedy)
1964	National League	Democrats (Lyndon Johnson)
1968	American League	Republican (Richard Nixon)

1972	American League	Republican (Richard Nixon)
1976	National League	Democrats (Jimmy Carter)

★ ★ ★

Clinton Shaw set the world's distance record for roller skating — 4,900 miles — by skating the Trans Canadian Highway from Victoria, British Columbia, to St. John's, Newfoundland, from April 1 to November 11, 1967.

★ ★ ★

Alf Dean, fishing at Denial Bay near Leduna, Australia, on April 21, 1959, hooked the largest fish ever caught on a rod, a 2,664-pound shark. It measured 16 feet, 10 inches in length.

★ ★ ★

From the time the National Hockey League was founded in 1917 until the early 1970's, players were traditionally Canadian-born. But in recent years, with interest skyrocketing in collegiate hockey in the United States, American-born players have begun to join the pro ranks in increasing numbers. Still, there is a lingering prejudice against Americans in some circles. Take the case of Robbie Ftorek. From Needham, Massachusetts, he was a legendary high school hockey player in the Boston area, and he starred for the United States Olympic team in Sapporo, Japan, in

1972. But he was overlooked in the National Hockey League draft. After he asked for a tryout with the Detroit Red Wings, they signed him to a one-year contract at a salary of $13,000, the minimum. The Wings released him after he had played in only 15 games, saying that he was too small. (Ftorek stands 5-foot-8; he weighs 150.)

Then Ftorek joined the Phoenix Roadrunners of the World Hockey Association. A forward, Ftorek became noted for his quickness and scoring ability, and for his hustling and aggressive style of play. In the 1976-77 season, he scored 117 points and was named the league's most valuable player. He was the first American-born player to win an MVP award in either the National Hockey League or the World Hockey Association.

★ ★ ★

For three seasons beginning in 1974, the Sacramento Solons of the Pacific Coast League played in one of baseball's most unusual parks. Named Hughes Stadium, it had a left-field foul line that was only 232 feet, 7 inches in length. (The major league minimum is 250 feet.) "We get home runs and wild plays in every game," said one official. "It's crazy." A team once hit 12 home runs in a game at Hughes Stadium. Two Sacramento players hit grand-slam home runs in the same inning. The score of an average game was 12-8. The Sacramento team once lost a game, 19-1. They once won, 24-14.

When a Sacramento pitcher hurled a homerless game, it was about the same as pitching a no hitter anywhere else. Naturally, Sacramento always led the league in home runs, and they led in attendance, too, proving that fans like pitching duels about as much as they like scoreless ties in football.

★ ★ ★

America's Edward Clark recorded the highest speed attained by a swimmer — 4.89 miles per hour — in a 25-yard pool at Yale University on March 26, 1964. Mark Spitz, by comparison, in setting the 100-meter record (50.47 seconds) in 1972, traveled at a speed of 4.34 miles an hour.

★ ★ ★

One of America's first sports heroes was a walker. His name was Edward Payson Weston. In 1867, at the age of 28, Weston made a bet of $10,000 that he could walk from Portland, Maine, to Chicago, Illinois — a distance of 1,326 miles — in 26 days. As he set out, he was trailed by six judges and dozens of newspaper reporters, all riding in horse-drawn vehicles. Weston walked the distance in 25 days, 22 hours, two hours under the deadline.

Weston's greatest walking feat took place in 1909. He walked from New York to California

— 3,895 miles — in 104 days. Then he turned around and walked back, taking only 77 days. Incredibly, Weston was 70 years old at the time.

★ ★ ★

During the 1968 season, the Dallas Tornados of the North American Soccer League set records that no other team envies. The Tornados won only two games, fewest in NASL history (a mark tied by Baltimore in 1969). The Dallas team lost 26 games, another record, and during one stretch went 22 games without a victory. A lack of defense was a chief reason for Dallas' poor showing. The team permitted a record 109 goals, an average of 3.4 goals per game.

★ ★ ★

In July, 1954, when Mildred (Babe) Didrikson arrived at the Salem (Massachusetts) Country Club to compete in the U. S. Women's Open, she was no longer the smiling, confident competitor she had once been. Cancer was ravaging her body and she did not have long to live. Few people believed she would be equal to a championship effort. But on the first two days of competition, Babe was superb, turning in a 72 and a 71. She led her closest rival by six strokes going into the final two rounds, both of which were to be played on the same day. Babe fired a 73 on the first round. The final 18 holes were torture for her, with pain dogging every step. But Babe refused to give in, finishing with a final round of 75. When she holed her last putt, she had to be helped from the course.

Not only did Babe win the 1954 Women's Open, but she won it by 12 strokes, the biggest margin ever achieved in a major golf event. Babe never played golf again, and within two years of her courageous victory she died.

★ ★ ★

On October 29, 1968, Mike Daugherty of Wooster, Ohio, bowled a game of 90, the highest in bowling history without a strike, spare, split, or foul being registered.

★ ★ ★

Pitcher Leon Cadore of the Brooklyn Dodgers and Joe Oeschger of the Boston Braves took the mound as rivals at Braves Field in Boston on the afternoon of May 1, 1920, and made baseball history. The Dodgers scored a run in the top half of the fifth inning. The Braves tied the score an inning later, and threatened in the bottom of the ninth, but failed to score. As inning followed inning, Cadore and Oeschger kept pitching, and zeroes kept going up on the scoreboard.

As play entered the 20th inning, darkness started to become a problem. Ball parks were not lighted in those days. The batters complained they could not see the ball. Finally, at the end of the 26th inning, umpire Barry McCormick halted the game. Cadore and Oeschger had pitched what amounted to almost three complete games. It was the longest game of all time.

Some of the newspaper reporters who covered the game predicted that the two men would never pitch again. But Oeschger was back on the mound eight days later. "I did miss one turn," he told *The Sporting News* in 1970. "I would have been ready to work in rotation, but the day after the game I pulled a muscle running around the park, and manager George Stallings let me skip my turn. But my arm was OK."

Oeschger won 15 games that season, and the next year, when he compiled a 20-14 record, was the best of his career. Cadore also won 15 games in 1920, the highest winning total of his career.

★ ★ ★

The first intercontinental automobile race of the 20th century was run in 1908 over a course that stretched from New York to Paris — but in the "wrong" direction, that is, from west to east. Times Square in New York City was the starting point. Six cars — three representing France; one, Germany; one, Italy; and one the United States — set out for San Francisco. From there, they sailed to Alaska and drove to the Bering Sea to be ferried across the Bering

Strait. Then it was across the continents of Asia and Europe. The United States car, a Thomas Flyer, won. Its winning time was 170 days, almost half a year.

★ ★ ★

Golf played with Frisbees? It's no pipe dream. The world's first Frisbee golf course opened in Pasadena, California, in August, 1975. Several such courses are now in operation. Spread over an expanse of about 20 acres, the 18-hole Pasadena layout compels players to shoot up and down hills; through, over, or around trees; and avoid out-of-bounds areas. The rules of golf apply. But instead of a green to putt on and a cup that's 4½ inches in diameter, the Frisbee course offers a metal basket welded to the top of a 4-foot steel pole. Par of 72 is bettered frequently, and the course record is 42.

★ ★ ★

At Grant Field In Atlanta, Georgia, on October 7, 1916, an angry Georgia Tech football team prepared to meet tiny Cumberland College of Williamsburg, Kentucky. The preceding spring Cumberland had humiliated Georgia Tech in baseball. Now Georgia Tech was eager for revenge. The first time Georgia Tech got possession of the ball, the team scored with ease. It soon became apparent that Cumberland was terribly overmatched. With the score 28-0 midway in the first quarter, Cumberland changed strategy. Instead of receiving the ball after a Tech touchdown, Cumberland elected to kick off, hoping to keep the opposition bottled up in its own half of the field. But the strategy backfired. At the end of the first period, Georgia Tech led, 63-0. At halftime, the score was 126-0.

When the second half got underway, the carnage continued. Georgia Tech boosted the score to 154-0 during the third quarter, establishing an all-time college record. Not long after, with the battered Cumberland players near exhaustion, the rival coaches agreed to halt the game. At the time, Georgia Tech was leading, 222-0.

★ ★ ★

When the Gallop Youth Survey polled teenagers in 1977 to learn the names of their favorite sports heroes, O. J. Simpson received more votes than anyone else. And there were more tennis players among the top 10 than athletes from any other sport. Here are the results of the poll:

1. O. J. Simpson (football)
2. Chris Evert (tennis)
3. Joe Namath (football)
4. Muhammad Ali (boxing)
5. Nadia Comaneci (gymnastics)
6. Julius Erving (basketball)
7. Billie Jean King (tennis)

8. Bruce Jenner (track and field)
9. Johnny Bench (baseball)
10. Jimmy Connors (tennis)

★ ★ ★

Harness-racing horses, called standardbreds, are bred for the purpose of pulling the light two-wheeled sulky and driver around the oval track at high speeds. Some harness horses are trained to trot, others to pace. A trotter moves its left front leg and right back leg simultaneously. A pacer moves both legs on the same side forward together.

★ ★ ★

The most one-sided game in the history of professional football was a league championship contest, played on December 8, 1940, which saw the Chicago Bears overpower the Washington Redskins, 73-0.

The game got so out of hand that after the ninth touchdown the referee explained to the Bears that they had kicked the game's supply of footballs into the stands on extra-point conversions, and that they should either pass or run on any succeeding extra-point attempts.

The victory was no fluke, for the following season the Bears swept to the championship of their division and took the league title again. They won the division crown for the third consecutive time in 1942, but lost in the league playoff. Ironically, the team that defeated them was the Washington Redskins.

★ ★ ★

Sports are often cited today for their rowdiness. But the most violent outburst of all time occurred almost a century ago, with the fans as much a part of the brawling as the players.

During a baseball game in Boston in May, 1894, the stormy John McGraw, then a third baseman with Baltimore, became involved in a punching match with Boston's Tom (Foghorn) Tucker. Players streamed from both dugouts to join in.

Then fights broke out in several places in the stands. In the midst of the fray, someone set fire to the bleachers. The flames spread to the grandstand and to buildings adjacent to the park. By the time the free-for-all ended and the flames had been doused, the ballpark was in ashes and more than 170 buildings had been damaged or destroyed.

★ ★ ★

Lee Trevino, winner of the U. S. Open in 1968 and 1971, and golf's leading money winner in 1970, once made a good portion of his living by betting on himself in matches in which he would devise unusual handicaps. His favorite was to use a Coke bottle instead of a set of regulation clubs in playing a round.

★ ★ ★

The Indianapolis 500, the most noted and most esteemed of American automobile races, has triggered many technical advances. One dates to 1911, the year the first "Indy" was held. All but one of the automobiles that year were two-seaters, permitting a passenger, a "riding mechanic" he was called, to sit alongside the driver and serve as a lookout. Roy Harroum, a late entrant, had the only single-seat car. To compensate for the fact that he had no one to keep watch for him during the race, Harroum fixed a small tripod to the car's hood to which he attached a 3-inch by 8-inch mirror. Harroum won the race that year, and in the years that followed, the rearview mirror, as it came to be called, became a standard piece of automobile equipment.

★ ★ ★

In ice hockey, jersey number 9 has taken on special significance, having been worn by some of the game's most noted players — Maurice Richard, Bobby Hull, and Gordie Howe. In professional football, the "star number" is number 32. It has been worn by Jim Brown and O. J. Simpson, the two greatest running backs in the sport's history.

★ ★ ★

O.J. Simpson

East Germany's sports program for women has been an unqualified success. In the 1976 Olympic Games, East German women won 57 of the country's 90 medals, or 63 percent. Of the 94 medals won by American athletes, only 17 were won by women, or 18 percent.

★ ★ ★

Ty Cobb is the only player in baseball to accumulate 4,000 hits. Cobb had 4,191 of them.

★ ★ ★

Larry Brown of the Washington Redskins, one of the most powerful and determined running backs of the 1970's, was unimpressive at training camp in his rookie season. One problem he had was that he was slow in getting off the mark. The ball would be in the quarterback's hands before Larry had even begun to move. It was then that coach Vince Lombardi discovered that Brown was nearly deaf in his right ear, and was not getting off with the snap because he didn't always hear the signals being called.

Lombardi's solution was to have a special helmet made for Brown with a hearing aid over the right ear. Not only did the device amplify the quarterback's signals, but it also helped Brown hear the footsteps of approaching tacklers.

Brown responded by averaging more than 1,000 yards rushing each year for the next five years, and he powered the Redskins into the Super Bowl in 1973. He now ranks as one of the best running backs in the team's history.

★ ★ ★

Paul Anderson, an American, lifted the greatest weight ever by a human, at Toccoa, Georgia, on June 12, 1957, when he raised 6,000 pounds.

★ ★ ★

During the final round of the 1934 U.S. Open Tournament, played at the famed Merion Country Club near Philadelphia, Bobby Cruickshank, an enthusiastic little Scotsman, battled for the lead. He came to the 11th hole, 370 yards in length, with a creek cutting across the fairway. When Cruickshank drove the ball and saw it head for the creek, he gasped in horror. But, incredibly, the ball hit a rock in the creek and rebounded onto the green. Cruickshank shrieked with joy and threw his club into the air. It came down to strike him on the head. The blow dazed him. When he resumed play, he was not able to regain his deft touch, and ended up in a tie for third place.

Dale Long, at 29, became the regular first baseman for the Pittsburgh Pirates in 1955. He batted .291 that season and hit an occasional home run. No one was prepared for his home-run outburst the next year. Beginning on May 19, 1956, Long hit a homer a game for eight consecutive games, setting a record no one has matched.

Strange happenings have marked the Olympic marathon event ever since it was first held in 1896. One of the strangest occurred in 1908. The events were held in London that year, with the 26-mile, 385-yard marathon course laid out from Windsor to the White City Stadium.

Italy's Dorando Pietri was the first of the 75 marathoners to enter the Stadium for the final lap. He started around the track — but in the wrong direction. Cries of the spectators and officials alerted him to his mistake. But no sooner had he reversed direction, than the exhausted Dorando collapsed. He struggled to his feet, ran a few steps, then collapsed again. It happened a third time, then a fourth, and a fifth.

J.M. Andrew, the chief clerk of the Olympics, and M.J. Bulger, a medical attendant, could not stand to see what they were watching. Rushing out onto the track, each man took Dorando by an arm and helped him through the final stages of the race and across the finish line. But their action caused Dorando to be disqualified, and the gold medal went to the second runner to cross the line, John Hayes, an American.

★ ★ ★

Newbern High School of Newbern, Tennessee, scored exactly 432 points in 432 minutes of football in 1952.

★ ★ ★

Soccer teams representing Wilmington Christian and Fairwinds Christian, two Delaware High schools, faced each other late in 1975. At the end of regulation play, the score was 1-1. The teams then sparred through two five-minute overtime periods without either scoring. A five-minute sudden-death overtime was scoreless, too. Then they tried another sudden-death overtime, and another, and another — 12 in all. Finally, after three hours of soccer and the score still deadlocked 1-1, the game was declared a tie. "A tie was a good way to end it," said the coach of the Fairwinds team. "We wouldn't want someone to win on a lucky shot after a game like that."

★ ★ ★

On May 4, 1975, when Bob Watson of the Houston Astros touched home plate, major league baseball, then in its 99th year, recorded its one-millionth run. When will the two-millionth run be scored? According to the Seiko Time Company, the event will take place on June 12, 2042.

★ ★ ★

Hocker may be the newest American game. It's simple and inexpensive, and can be played on an equal basis by participants of both sexes, and by people of different sizes and assorted skills. Hocker was thought up by John Henry Norton of Fairfield, Connecticut, the father of 14 children, who wanted a game that they all could play together.

As the game's name may suggest, hocker is a blend of hockey and soccer. The ball is a soft rubber playground ball, 16 inches in diameter. The field is the size of a football field, but it can be smaller. It's surrounded by a four-foot-high fence so the ball won't go out of play.

Each side has nine players. Points in value from one to five are scored by sending the ball through or over the single set of goalposts from the front or back.

Once play begins, it seldom stops. You move the ball by passing or kicking it. You can also punch it or butt it with your head. What you can't do is hold it. There are no field markings, no offsides.

Seven points are needed to win a set, which takes about 15 minutes to play. The match goes to the team winning the greatest number of an agreed upon number of sets. Norton, who spent 10 years developing the game, looks for it to spread from the lawn of his Fairfield, Connecticut, estate to parks and playgrounds across the country.

★ ★ ★

In the years he spent with the Boston Bruins of the National Hockey League, Phil Esposito established countless scoring records that may never be matched. Bobby Hull of the Chicago Black Hawks was the game's goal-scoring leader in an earlier era. But neither Hull nor Esposito ever came close to equaling a performance by Joe Malone of the Quebec Bulldogs on January 31, 1920. In a game at Quebec City, Malone scored a record seven goals in Quebec's 10-6 victory over the Toronto St. Patricks. No player before or since has had

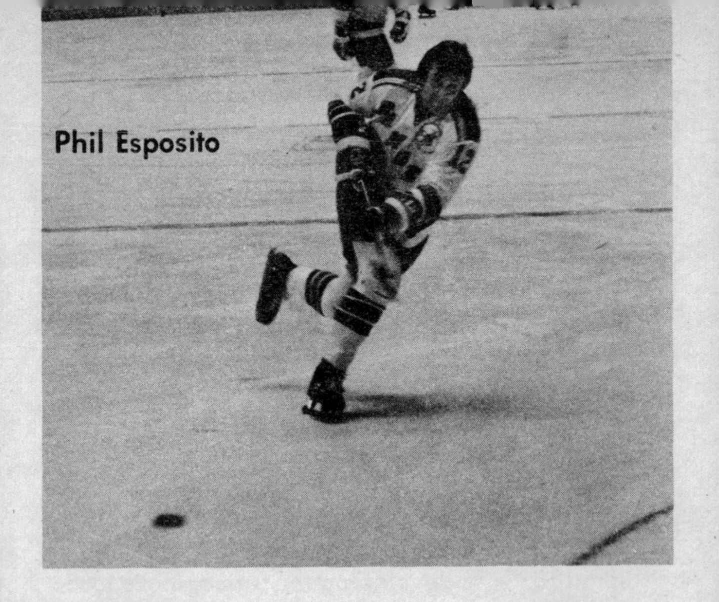
Phil Esposito

a seven-goal game. Just a few weeks later, as if to show his outburst was no fluke, Malone scored six goals in a game against the Ottawa Senators. Only five other players have had six-goal games. Red Berenson of the St. Louis Blues, who scored six goals against the Philadelphis Flyers on November 7, 1968, was the player who last accomplished the feat.

★ ★ ★

The largest field for any ball is that for polo. At its maximum, it is 300 yards long and 220 yards wide — an area of 12.4 acres.

★ ★ ★

While Jackie Robinson, who joined the

Brooklyn Dodgers in 1947, is generally acknowledged as being the first black major league baseball player, some sources accord that recognition to Moses (Fleet) Walker. Walker was a catcher for Toledo of the American Association, a rival league to the National League, during the season of 1884. From Mt. Pleasant, Ohio, Walker played in 41 games and batted .251.

★ ★ ★

Students at Barrow, Alaska, High School who enjoy playing sports also have to enjoy traveling. Their road trips are major expeditions. Barrow, population 1,314, is located in northernmost Alaska, on the shore of the Arctic Ocean. Barrow High is the only high school in the North Slope Borough, which covers an area of over 88,000 square miles, larger than the state of Kansas. Of the 110 students attending the school, well over half compete on Barrow's basketball, track, volleyball, wrestling, badminton, and gymnastic teams. Barrow's nearest rivals are in Nome and Fairbanks, each a 1,000-mile round trip. Barrow's teams journey 27,000 miles a year to find opponents.

★ ★ ★

Spiked shoes were introduced at a track meet at the Empire Skating Rink in New York on November 11, 1868. They were worn by William B. Curtis in winning a 75-yard race. Before the meet ended, Curtis' shoes were borrowed by four other athletes and used in seven different events.

★ ★ ★

Unlimited hydroplane racing has been called the water version of the Indianapolis 500. Races are conducted in the United States in Detroit, Miami, Washington, D.C., Seattle, and the tiny community of Madison, Indiana, where as many as 100,000 people attend the Madison Regatta each year.

Over the past 20 years or so, the sport has been dominated by Bill Muncey, although to use the word *dominate* is to actually understate his status. Muncey has not had a serious challenger for the position of preeminence he holds. In 1976, Muncey's 21st year of serious competition, he captured a record fifth national unlimited hydroplane driving championship. In those 21 years, Muncey raced 147 times, won 38 times, and placed third or better 75 times. No other driver has won more than 20 races.

★ ★ ★

Up until the late 1960's, most teams of the National Hockey League carried only one goalie, and he played every minute of every game. If cut, he was stitched up and sent back out onto the ice. But the greater number of games that teams now play forced a change, a switch to the two-goalie system. For this reason, a record compiled by Glenn Hall, who played for the Detroit Red Wings and later the Chicago Black Hawks, seems unbeatable. Beginning with the first game of the 1955-56 season through the 12th game of the 1962-63 season, Hall was in the net for a record 502 consecutive games. On November 7, 1962, in his 503rd straight game, Hall injured his back and was forced to go to the bench.

★ ★ ★

Just about every baseball fan is aware of Joe DiMaggio's record of hitting in 56 consecutive games, established in 1941. Less well known is the record for consecutive hits. It's 12, and it's shared by two men — Pinkey Higgins of the Boston Red Sox and Walt Dropo of the Detroit Tigers. Higgins, in 1938, was the first to get 12 hits in a row. Dropo followed in 1952.

★ ★ ★

During the 1899 season, the undefeated University of the South football team from Sewanee, Tennessee, undertook the task of playing in five different cities in a span of six days against five of the most powerful college teams of the day. In the first game, Sewanee defeated Texas University at Austin, Texas, then traveled by horse and wagon to the town of College Station, Texas, where they met and defeated Texas A & M. In New Orleans, the very next day, Sewanee defeated Tulane University. The following day, a Sunday, the Sewanee players rested. On Monday, Sewanee trimmed undefeated Louisiana State University, and the next day crossed into Mississippi and whipped Mississippi State University.

Sewanee had played and won five football games against five major opponents in six days. What's astonishing about the achievement is that the Sewanee squad numbered only 11 players. The amazing victory string was achieved without the use of a single substitute.

★ ★ ★

The youngest golfer ever to win the U.S. Open Championship was an Englishman, Horace Rawlins. In 1895, the year he captured the Open title at Newport, Rhode Island, Rawlins was 19 years old.

★ ★ ★

In a National Hockey League game between the Toronto Maple Leafs and the Pittsburgh Penguins on October 16, 1968, Jim Dorey of the Leafs distinguished himself in an undistinguished manner, committing infractions that added up to nine penalties (four minor penalties, two major penalties, two 10-minute misconduct penalties, and one game misconduct penalty) for a total of 48 penalty minutes.

Seven of the penalties were called during one period, the game's second period.

★ ★ ★

A baseball player's slugging average is probably a truer indication of his power at the plate than any other statistic. The figure is arrived at by dividing a player's at-bats into his total bases. A man who hits a home run on every official at-bat would have a slugging average of 4.000.

Babe Ruth holds virtually all of baseball's slugging records, including the highest slugging average for a season (.847 in 1920), and the highest career slugging average (.690).

★ ★ ★

Athletes are generally at their best between the ages of 27 and 29, according to an article titled, "The Most Proficient Years at Sports and Games," by Professor Harvey C. Lehman of Ohio University.

However, the years of peak performance can vary widely, depending upon the sport, said Professor Lehman. He found that baseball players are likely to reach their peak years at the age of 27, and that they maintain peak effectiveness for a span of 4.39 years. Professional football players and hockey players begin their peak years earlier, at age 24. Football players stay at their top level for only 2.33 years, the shortest time span of all athletes. In bowling, competitors don't become their best until the relatively advanced age of 37.

★ ★ ★

The term "Grand Slam" was used to describe golfer Bobby Jones' amazing four victories in 1930 when he won the American and British Open Championships and the American and British Amateur Championships. More recently, the term has been used to describe the four major professional events — the United States and British Open Championships, the Masters Tournament, and the Professional Golfers' Association Tournament. But no matter which description is used, Bobby Jones still ranks as the only golfer to have ever pulled off a "Grand Slam."

★ ★ ★

On July 30, 1968, in a game against the Cleveland Indians, Ron Hansen, shortstop for the Washington Senators, caught a line drive off the bat of Joe Azcue, stepped on second base to retire Dave Nelson, then tagged Russ Snyder coming in from first, thus completing an unassisted triple play. None has occurred since, and only seven other unassisted triple plays had taken place in all of baseball history. The triple play, in terms of rarity, ranks with the perfect game.

Of the eight unassisted triple plays that have occurred, five were executed by shortstops, two by first basemen, and one by a second baseman. All were made with runners on first and second base — only. Two were made on successive days — May 30 and 31, 1927.

★ ★ ★

Petaluma, California, bills itself as the arm-wrestling capital of the world.

★ ★ ★

Heavyweight boxer Jack Doyle, nicknamed the "Irish Thrush" because he liked to sing Irish songs, perhaps should have chosen singing as his profession. In the second round of a bout with Eddie Phillips, Doyle threw a roundhouse right that missed Phillips completely. His momentum carried Doyle through the ropes. Before he landed on the arena floor, he struck his head on the ring apron, knocking himself out. The referee counted 10, and the fight was over.

★ ★ ★

Mike Winter, goalkeeper for the St. Louis Stars of the North American Soccer League, turned in one of the sport's most frenzied performances in a game against the Rochester Lancers on May 27, 1973. The Stars' porous defense caused Hunter to make 22 saves, an NASL record.

★ ★ ★

Who had the fastest fastball of all time? No one knows for sure, of course. But in 1974 two of Nolan Ryan's pitches were timed at 100.8 and 100.9 miles per hour by scientists of the Rockwell International Corporation. Bob Feller, who had an exceptional career as a fastballer for the Cleveland Indians for two decades beginning in 1936, had ranked earlier as the fastest pitcher on record, with a throw timed at 98.6 miles an hour.

★ ★ ★

Mark Warrilow opened up a 100- x 120-foot public swimming pool in a London suburb not long ago, filled it with half a million gallons of water, and waited for the crowds to come. They never did. The pool was unheated and the summer was cold. But Warrilow managed to save himself from a financial drowning by dumping loads of sand and gravel into the pool until the bottom was covered. Then he stocked it with trout. Anglers by the hundreds lined up for the privilege of trying out the new fishing hole.

★ ★ ★

Graceful, fleet-footed Wilma Rudolph scored a rare double victory in the 1960 Olympic Games, winning the 100-meter dash in 11 seconds, and the 200-meter dash in 24 sec-

Nolan Ryan

onds. And when she anchored the American team to a victory and an Olympic record in the 400-meter relay, she also became the only track or field athlete to win as many as three gold medals in the 1960 Olympics, and the first American woman ever to reign as a triple winner.

★ ★ ★

In his long career with the Detroit Red Wings, Gordie Howe set several National Hockey League records, some of which may never be broken. These are among them:

Most seasons, 25
Most games, 1,687
Most goals, 786
Most assists, 1,023
Most points, 1,809
Most games, including playoffs, 1,841
Most goals, including playoffs, 853
Most assists, including playoffs, 1,114
Most points, including playoffs, 1,967

There was one other statistic associated with Howe's career that should be mentioned. He collected some 500 facial stitches.

★ ★ ★

Lou Gehrig's record of playing in 2,130 consecutive games, compiled from 1925 to 1939, is probably as unbreakable as any baseball record can be. An idea of what Gehrig accomplished can be derived by comparing his record with the consecutive-game record in the National League. Held by the Cubs' Bill Williams, it's a mere 1,117 games.

★ ★ ★

During the early to mid-1970's, Dave Schultz of the Philadelphia Flyers of the National Hockey League was recognized as the sport's toughest tough guy. It's a reputation that the record book confirms. Schultz spent almost eight full hours in penalty boxes during the 1974-75 season, a record 472 minutes. The record he broke — 348 minutes — was his own, established in 1973-74.

★ ★ ★

One of the strangest goofs on the part of football officials came during a game between the Los Angeles Rams and Chicago Bears several years ago when a member of the sideline crew inadvertently gave the down marker an extra flip. The Rams were in possession of the ball at the time, but no one on the team noticed they had been robbed of a down. Nor was the error caught by any of the other officials, by any of the players or coaches on the sidelines, by any one of the 80,000 fans who were on hand, or by the press. Only afterward, when the play-by-play account of the game was being reviewed, did someone discover the missed call.

For sheer endurance on the basketball court, a special award should have gone to the players who participated in the game between the Indianapolis Olympians and the Rochester Royals on January 6, 1951. It took a record six overtime contests to decide the game, Indianapolis finally winning, 75-73.

When the Cincinnati Reds won the National League pennant in 1972, much of the credit went to Sparky Anderson, the team's canny manager, and to such standout players as Johnny Bench, Pete Rose, and Joe Morgan. Some people felt that Dr. John Nash deserved a pat on the back, too. It was Dr. Nash, the author of a book titled *Health and Light* that evaluated the effect of light on humans, who prescribed that the underside of the bills of the Reds' caps be changed from green to gray.

The Indianapolis 500 is one of the best attended sports events in the world. More than 300,000 people turn out for the event each year. They leave behind an estimated 6.6 million pounds of trash. The race itself takes just over three hours to complete. The clean-up job requires 10 days.

★ ★ ★

Owners of professional sports franchises sometimes pick out training sites that are known more for their remoteness than anything else, the idea being to remove players from any possible source of temptation. The Green Bay Packers, for instance, train at De Pere, Wisconsin. The New England Patriots get tucked away in Smithfield, Rhode Island. Baseball's Chicago Cubs used to go to Catalina Island off the coast of California, and the Brooklyn Dodgers once hid away in the Dominican Republic. But the Toronto Toros of the World Hockey Association once picked the remotest site of all. In 1975, the team trained at Ornskoldsvik in Sweden. The site was 300 miles from Stockholm and almost 4,000 miles from the team's home base in Toronto.

★ ★ ★

After John Walker set a new mile record in August, 1975, turning in a time of 3 minutes, 49.4 seconds for the event, theorists again began to speculate what times runners of the future might record for the event. *Sports Illustrated* pointed out that over the previous century the mile record dropped by an average of 3½ seconds per decade. The magazine forecast that the record could drop to 3 minutes, 42 seconds by 1985; to 3 minutes, 40 seconds by 1995; and to 3 minutes, 38 seconds early in the 21st century.

★ ★ ★

"Ed Cook, left halfback for Oklahoma University, swam 10 yards for the first touchdown of the game with A & M College of Stillwater at Island Park yesterday afternoon, a thing which perhaps never occurred before." That's how the *Oklahoma State Capitol*, in its edition dated November 6, 1904, began the account of one of the most bizarre games in football history.

Indeed, swimming for a touchdown had never occurred before. It surely has not happened since.

The game took place in Guthrie, Oklahoma, on a cold and cloudy afternoon. Early in the first quarter, in possession of the ball on their own one-foot line, the Aggies were forced to punt from their end zone. The ball shot straight up in the air. Carried by a strong wind, it sailed back to fall into a creek that ran through the end zone. Several players plunged into the water after it. As they scrambled, the game resembled water polo more than football. Ed Cook, an Oklahoma halfback, finally captured the ball and waded ashore to touch it down in the A & M end zone. Later in the game, Cook showed his versatility by scoring a second touchdown on an 80-yard run. It was an easy victory for the University of Oklahoma team. After the game, the University newspaper noted, "If Stillwater expects to play football with our boys on a creek bank, she must teach her fellows to swim...."

★ ★ ★

Most baseball players play no more than two or three positions during their careers. Occasionally a player will be so versatile he will be used in most of the infield and outfield positions, and there have been some players who played all nine positions during their careers. There are two players who were used at every position during a single game. The two are Bert Campaneris, who played all nine positions for the Kansas City A's on September 9, 1965, and Cesar Tovar, who did it for the Minnesota Twins on September 22, 1968.

★ ★ ★

During the period from December 3, 1929, through January 9, 1930, the Boston Bruins ran up the longest winning streak in National Hockey League history — 14 games. The Bruins also own hockey's longest undefeated streak — 23 games — a record compiled from December 22, 1940, through February 23, 1941. It consists of 15 victories and eight ties.

★ ★ ★

In January, 1950, the Associated Press polled

393 sports editors, columnists, writers, and broadcasters throughout the United States to find out whom they considered to be the greatest athletes of the first half of the 20th century in each of 13 different categories. Here are the results of the voting:

Baseball	Babe Ruth
Football	Jim Thorpe
Boxing	Jack Dempsey
Tennis	Bill Tilden
Track	Jesse Owens
Golf	Bobby Jones
Swimming	Johnny Weissmuller
Basketball	George Mikan
Greatest Male Athlete	Jim Thorpe
Greatest Female Athlete	Babe Didrikson Zaharias

★ ★ ★

It is universally held that the 4-foot-11, 102-pound Willie Shoemaker is the greatest jockey of all time. No one else is even close to him.

On a Sunday afternoon at Santa Anita racetrack in California during March, 1976, the 44-year-old Shoemaker won aboard Royal Derby II, posting the 7,000th victory of his 28-year career. He thus became the first rider in American turf history to win 7,000 races. The No. 2 man on the list, the retired Johnny Longden, had 6,026 winners.

Of Shoemaker's 7,000 victories, 111 came in races worth $100,000 or more. He won the Kentucky Derby three times. He rode six winners in one day on nine different occasions. The 483 winners he rode in 1953 stood as a record for 20 years. His mounts earned a total of almost $60,000,000. Since jockeys get to keep 10 percent of their mounts' earnings, Shoemaker ranks as one of the highest paid sports figures of all time.

The most difficult of the Grand Prix automobile races is The Monaco, a lap event conducted over a 1.95-mile route through the streets of Monte Carlo. The course has 10 sharp corners and several steep changes in grade, which make necessary some 1,500 gear changes. The lap record is 1 minute, 34.5 seconds (74.4 miles per hour), established by John Surtees of England on May 26, 1963. Surtees drove a Ferrari.

Richard Caplette of Danielson, Connecticut, earned a niche in the American Bowling Congress's official record manual, and the warm sympathy of the bowling world when, on September 7, 1971, he rolled 19 gutter balls in a single game. His score for the game was 3, the lowest ever recorded in sanctioned league play.

★ ★ ★

For baseball trivia buffs, the town of New Ulm, Minnesota, has special significance. New Ulm is to pitchers with infinite earned-run-averages what the state of Kentucky is to thoroughbreds. An infinite earned-run-average is achieved by a pitcher who yields one or more earned runs without retiring a single batter during his career. According to *The Baseball Encyclopedia,* 11 major league pitchers have had the unenviable distinction of compiling infinite earned-run-averages since 1900. And two of them, Elmer (Doc) Hamann of the 1922 Cleveland Indians and Fred Bruckbauer of the 1961 Minnesota Twins, were both born in New Ulm, giving the town a monopoly on the specialty. Except for Hamann and Bruckbauer, no other major league pitchers were born in New Ulm.

★ ★ ★

Wilt Chamberlain, Bill Russell, and Kareem Abdul-Jabbar, three of basketball's most noted "giants," have each had an important influence on how the game is played. When Chamberlain began his college career at the University of Kansas, and an opponent's shot hovered on the basket's rim, Wilt would jump up and knock the ball away. This practice is known as goaltending, and it's now forbidden.

Bill Russell, as a college player at the University of San Francisco, liked to station him-

Kareem Abdul-Jabbar
(Lew Alcindor)

self just to the right or left of the basket to pluck off rebounds. He got to be so good at it that the rules-makers widened the free-throw lane from six feet to 12 feet, and rebounding — offensive rebounding, that is — became more challenging for Russell and everyone else.

When Kareem Abdul-Jabbar, then known as Lew Alcindor, arrived upon the scene at UCLA, he brought with him his spectacular dunk shot. He would leap high into the air to stuff the ball *down* through the basket. College officials were quick to outlaw the dunk, although it again became legal in 1976-77. The dunk has always been permitted in the pro ranks.

★ ★ ★

The longest match in the history of U.S. Tennis Association competition took place on February 16, 1968, at the U.S. Indoor Championships at Salisbury, Maryland. A doubles match in which England's Mark Cox and Robert K. Wilson defeated America's Charles Pasarell and Ron Holmburg, 26-24, 17-19, 30-28, lasted 6 hours, 23 minutes.

★ ★ ★

Traditionally, high jumpers use either the Western roll or the straddle jump in getting over the bar. In both styles, the approach is slow and deliberate. The foot closest to the bar is the take-off foot, and the body is parallel to the bar as it passes over it.

★ ★ ★

In 1888, J.B. Dunlop, an English veterinary surgeon, developed the pneumatic tire, which triggered a period of mushrooming growth for the bicycle industry. Bike racing soon became popular in almost every country of the world. Amateur races in the United States were often held on sidewalks, because the roads in those days were not paved, and thus usually deeply rutted. The race riders, known as scorchers, were responsible for countless pedestrian casualties. The situation led to the passage of laws, still on the books in many states, which forbid the use of bicycles on sidewalks.

Pro football's No. 1 draft choice invariably signs a contract that guarantees him that he'll be earning money by the helmetful. Such wasn't the case with the very first of the No. 1 choices — Jay Berwanger, a running back from the University of Chicago in 1936. Berwanger was also the first player to win the Heisman Trophy. After being drafted by the Chicago Bears, Berwanger asked for a two-year contract at $12,500 a year. That was more than George Halas, the owner of the Bears, was willing to pay, so Berwanger entered the business world and never played professional football.

Which players will lead the major leagues in batting this year? The Puerto Rican Winter League may furnish a tipoff. The batting champion in Puerto Rico almost always becomes a prominent player in the United States, and frequently repeats his league-leading batting performance. There are countless examples. Willie Mays was the batting champion in the Puerto Rican League in 1955, and Roberto Clemente won the title in 1957. Tony Oliva won it in 1964, and Tony Perez in 1967. More recent winners include Don Baylor in

1972, Ken Griffey in 1975, and Dan Driessen in 1976.

Sixto Lezcano, an outfielder for the Milwaukee Brewers, won the Puerto Rican batting championship in 1977 with a sizzling .366. Lezcano had never hit as much as .300 as a major leaguer, and few baseball fans outside of Milwaukee knew his name. But if form holds true, he may be a star performer one day.

★ ★ ★

In their book, *The Search for a Perfect Swing*, authors Alastair Cochran and John Stobbs report that a good drive in golf springs from the clubhead at a speed of about 200 feet a second, or 136 miles per hour, and requires a clubhead speed of about 100 miles per hour.

★ ★ ★

Many basketball experts agree that Wilt Chamberlain was the most dominating force pro basketball has known. A glance at the National Basketball Association's record book confirms this. Chamberlain is the only player in the history of the game to have exceeded 30,000 points for his career (his total: 31,419 points) and 4,000 points for a season (he scored 4,029 points in 1961-62).

In a game at Hershey, Pennsylvania, on March 2, 1962, Chamberlain scored 100 points, the league record. The second highest point total by one player in a single game is 78 —

also by Chamberlain. In fact, in the listing of players who have scored the most points in one game, 15 of the first 16 entries belong to Wilt the Stilt.

During the 1961-62 season, Chamberlain averaged 50.4 points in one game, another record. In a game during the 1965-66 season, he once scored 15 consecutive points. He is the league's all-time leader in rebounds, with 23,924 of them. In one game he grabbed a record 55 rebounds.

But when Chamberlain stepped to the foul line to attempt a free throw, he often looked like a rank amateur. He was successful in a mere 51 percent of his foul shots during his 14-year career. (Coaches want their players to make at least 75 percent of their shots from the free-throw line.) Chamberlain tried every free-throw style. He tried shooting from several inches in back of the line. But his inability to be consistent from the free-throw line dogged him from the beginning of his career to the very end.

Chamberlain's inability from the foul line is documented by the National Basketball Association records that he holds:

- Most free throws missed, season — 578 (1967-68)

- Most free throws missed, game — 22 (Philadelphia vs. Seattle, December 1, 1967)

- Most free throws missed, playoff game — 17 (Philadelphia vs. Boston, April 12, 1966)

★ ★ ★

In professional hockey, the prize for ineptitude has to go to the Kansas City Scouts. During the National Hockey League's 1975-76 season, the Scouts managed to win only 12 of 80 games (losing 56, tying 12). The last 44 games of the season were the dreariest of all for the Scouts, for they won only once.

★ ★ ★

The first baseball game ever televised was a college game between Columbia and Princeton at Baker Field in New York City on May 17, 1939. Bill Stern was the announcer. Later that year the first football game was telecast. It, too, was a college game. It was played at Randall's Island in New York City on September 30 between Fordham University and Waynesburg College. On February 28, 1940, Fordham participated in the first televised basketball game. It took place at Madison Square Garden. The University of Pittsburgh furnished the opposition. The first hockey game to be televised was also played at Madison Square Garden. The date was February 25, 1940. The New York Rangers and the Montreal Canadiens were the opposing teams. In each of the above instances, it was station W2XBS that did the televising.

★ ★ ★

Barrel jumping, a sport in which ice skaters attempt to clear wooden barrels that are lying on their sides, is believed to have originated in the 1600's in Holland, where skating of all types is pursued. James Papreck of Northbrook, Illinois, established the world record for barrel jumping when, in 1975, he cleared 16 barrels, a distance of 29 feet, 4 inches.

★ ★ ★

During the 1970-71 National Hockey League season, when Phil Esposito, who then played for the Boston Bruins, set an all-time scoring record of 76 goals, he also established the record for most shots. Esposito fired the puck at the goal 550 times that season, an average of slightly more than seven times per game.

★ ★ ★

The largest crowd ever to attend a professional sports event turned out for soccer's World Cup final game between Brazil and Uruguay in Rio de Janeiro, Brazil, on July 16, 1950. According to the official count, 199,854 fans attended the match, which was won by Uruguay.

★ ★ ★

Jennifer Amyx of Woodsboro, Maryland, became the first five-year-old girl to finish a marathon (a distance of 26 miles, 385 yards), when she competed in the Johnstown, Pennsylvania, Marathon in November, 1975. She placed 66 in the event, with a time of 4 hours, 56 minutes, 35 seconds.

★ ★ ★

When 42-year-old A. J. Foyt roared away from the starting line in his 20th consecutive Indianapolis 500 in 1977, he added to a longevity record that was unequaled for the event. Foyt entered his first 500 in 1958, and of the 33 drivers who started that race, he was the only one still active in racing. And two of Foyt's rivals in 1977 — Gary Bettenhausen and Johnny Parsons — were sons of men that Foyt had driven against in 1958. During the ensuing 20 years, Foyt has been the fastest qualifier four times, has led the race a record 10 times, and has won it four times — in 1961, 1964, 1967, and 1977.

★ ★ ★

In his 23-year career with the old Milwaukee Braves, then with the Atlanta Braves, and finally the two seasons he spent as the designated hitter for the Milwaukee Brewers, Hank Aaron smashed two of baseball's most noted records. He surpassed Babe Ruth's all-time home-run record of 714, ending his career with

Hank Aaron

755 homers, and he broke Ruth's career RBI record of 2,216, finishing with 2,297.

That's not all that Aaron accomplished by any means. He established major-league records for games played (3,298) and total bases (6,856). He won two National League batting championships (in 1956 and 1959), four National League home-run titles (in 1957, 1963, 1966, and 1967), and four RBI championships (in 1957, 1960, 1963, and 1966). He was named the league's Most Valuable Player in 1957.

Aaron's final season was 1976. In the last of his record 12,364 at-bats, Aaron produced a base hit that drove in a run. When he was removed from the game for a pinch hitter, he received a standing ovation from the crowd of 6,858 at Milwaukee's County Stadium. At the time, Aaron was tied with Babe Ruth for second place on career runs scored. Each had 2,174. Ty Cobb, with 2,245, was the leader. After the game, Aaron admitted he would have liked to have broken the tie with Ruth. "I would have loved to have another run," he said. "But I don't want to get into any controversy. My career is done — over with. Let it go at that."

★ ★ ★

Switching football to the metric system shouldn't be difficult. Dr. Andrew Hulsebosch of the Eastern Analysis Institute has suggested 90-meter football, that is, playing the game on a field that measures 90 meters in length and 50 meters in width. Such a field would be only 1½ yards shorter between the goal lines than the present field, and about 2½ yards wider.

Of course, there'd be no "first down and 10 yards to go" situations. Instead, Dr. Hulsebosch suggests striping the field every five meters. There would still be a first and 10, but it would be first and 10 meters (10 yards, 2 feet, 10 inches).

★ ★ ★

During one recent year, seven schools in suburban Chicago kept track of the injuries sustained in nine different sports, the idea being to determine which sports were the most hazardous. One sport led all the others by a wide margin. It was volleyball, with 31.4 percent of the students reporting that they had been injured in that sport. Football, with 10.9 percent, was a distant second. Gymnastics, with 9.3 percent, was third. Wrestling, soccer, basketball, tennis, golf, and track followed in that order.

★ ★ ★

Field hockey is a sport with many of the characteristics of ice hockey, soccer, and basketball — sports in which men have traditionally excelled. Yet on an international basis, field hockey is one sport in which women have consistently outshone men.

The United States Field Hockey Association, an organization of women field-hockey players, was founded in 1922. The Field Hockey Association of America, the men's organization, didn't come into existence until 1930.

★ ★ ★

On November 8, 1970, Tom Dempsey, then a member of the New Orleans Saints, booted the longest field goal in pro football history, a 63-yard kick that carried his team to a 19-17 victory over the Detroit Lions. The kick was seven yards farther than the previous longest kick. One can come to an appreciation of the great distance involved by realizing that the ball was booted from the New Orleans 37-yard line, or three yards farther back than the 40-yard line, the kickoff point at the time.

Dempsey, who was later to play for the Philadelphia Eagles and the Los Angeles Rams, was born handicapped, with half a right foot, his kicking foot. He also had only a stub for a right hand. He wore a special kicking shoe, only 6½ inches in length, and so constructed as to offer a rectangular kicking surface, about 3 inches long and 2 inches wide. The shoe laced at the side. The shoe he used in booting his record kick is on display at the Pro Football Hall of Fame in Canton, Ohio.

★ ★ ★

Pete Gray, an outfielder with the St. Louis Browns in 1945, earned lasting fame although he played in only 77 games and batted a mere .218. Gray had only one arm.

★ ★ ★

When the National Table Tennis League set up shop in 1975, officials unveiled an official table to be used in all matches. Gone was the familiar green paint job, replaced by bright blue and red stripes. And instead of a single sheet of plywood, the new table was constructed of laminated layers of wood surrounding a hollow aluminum core. Microphones implanted within the core amplified the sounds of balls striking the surface, the idea being to sharpen player response. Despite all of the improvements, the public did not rush to buy the new table. Perhaps its $25,000 price tag was the reason.

★ ★ ★

The marathon, the longest footrace on the Olympic program, is named after the ancient Greek city of Marathon. The distance of the race — 26 miles, 385 yards — is exactly the same as the distance from Marathon to the Greek capital of Athens.

The event is meant to commemorate the heroic feat of a Greek soldier named Pheidippides who, in 490 B.C., ran from Marathon to Athens bringing news of the Greek army's triumph over the hordes of invading Persians. With his announcement, "Rejoice, we conquer," Pheidippides dropped dead.

★ ★ ★

On March 30, 1968, Henry Dancyger of Brooklyn, New York, became the third person in bowling history to record a 698 three-game series—without bowling a 200 game. He did it—as the others did—on games of 199, 300, and 199.

★ ★ ★

Almost every sports event has a dramatic moment or two, and some have several. How could anyone possibly select the most dramatic moment in sports history? The Associated Press attempted to do so in 1950, limiting the choice to events that occurred in the first half of the 20th century. Of the 318 sports experts polled, 70 of them, about 24 percent, selected the Jack Dempsey-Luis Firpo fight. It took place in New York City on September 14, 1927. Dempsey, the world champion at the time, had already won recognition as the greatest fighter of all time. Firpo, 6-foot-3, 220 pounds, from Argentina, and known as the Wild Bull of the Pampas, was a formidable challenger. The more than 88,000 fans who jammed the Polo Grounds witnessed one of the most savage bouts in history. It lasted only 3 minutes, 57 seconds.

In the first round, Dempsey knocked Firpo down several times. But as the round was coming to a close, an enraged Firpo connected with a hard right to Dempsey's jaw that sent him through the ropes and into the laps of newsmen. Friends pushed Dempsey back into the ring at the count of nine, saving him from defeat. In the second round, Dempsey sent Firpo to the floor again with devastating body punches, then knocked him out with a powerful right to the jaw.

★ ★ ★

Baseball has a rich history. There's even a tradition for the enormous amounts of money that modern players receive. It dates to 1915, the year that William (Duke) Kenworthy, a second baseman for the Kansas City team of the old Federal League, bent down to pick up a pebble that had made a ground ball bounce over his head. The pebble was a solid gold nugget, making Kenworthy the wealthiest player of his day.

Dave DeBusschere, commissioner of the American Basketball Association at the time of its merger with the National Basketball Association in 1976, had a remarkable career as a player. Through 12 active seasons, the 6-foot-6 DeBusschere, a forward, played in eight All-Star games and was a member of championship teams with the New York Knicks in 1970 and 1973. At the same time, he also performed as a pitcher in the Chicago White Sox system, and in 1962 and 1963 he pitched for the parent club.

Gary Gabelich, driving *The Blue Flame* (37 feet in length, powered by liquid natural gas), established the land-speed record for wheeled vehicles on October 23, 1970, when he whisked over the Bonneville Salt Flats of Utah at a speed of 627.287 miles per hour. An earlier run that day was timed at 617.602 m.p.h., giving Gabelich an average speed of 622.407 m.p.h.

During one of the runs, a speed of 650 m.p.h. was briefly achieved.

★ ★ ★

Amos Alonzo Stagg, who died in 1965 at the age of 103, was the dean of football coaches, and responsible for countless innovations that have become accepted practice. Stagg used the first pass-or-run option plays and he introduced the huddle. He was the first to use the place kick, a departure from the drop kick. He made major contributions in the development of the T-formation. One of his little known inventions was the tackling dummy. In the gymnasium at Yale University in the fall of 1889, Stagg rolled up a mattress, suspended it from the ceiling, and ordered his players to block and tackle it.

★ ★ ★

A tennis service by England's Michael Sangster, measured in June, 1963, was determined to have crossed the net at a speed of 108 miles an hour.

★ ★ ★

During the season of 1973, Bob Rigby of the Philadelphia Atoms of the North American Soccer League established himself as pro soccer's finest goalkeeper, allowing a mere eight goals during the season, an average of .062

goals per game. Both are season records that still stand.

★ ★ ★

Steve Dalkowski may have been baseball's hardest thrower of all time, but he never reached the major leagues. His chronic wildness kept him in the minors, where he set records for both strikeouts and bases-on-balls. Earl Weaver, who managed the Baltimore Orioles through most of the 1970's, saw Dalkowski pitch, and believed him to be the fastest thrower of all time. "He'd come right over the top with the ball," Weaver once said, "and it would rise as much as six inches. I honestly believe he was faster than Nolan Ryan."

Once in 1958, an effort was made to time Dalkowski's fastball. But it took almost 40 minutes for him to get his pitches within range of the timing devices, and by that time he was beginning to tire. Still, one of his throws was recorded at a speed of 93.5 miles an hour.

★ ★ ★

Golf was a humble sport indulged in by only a handful of participants at the time of the U.S. Open in 1913. It was played at the Brookline Country Club in Brookline, Massachusetts. The tournament ended in a three-way tie involving England's Harry Vardon and Ted Ray, the leading professionals of the day, and an "unknown" American, 20-year-old Francis

Ouimet, a lanky, sad-eyed former caddy who lived across the street from the Brookline course. In the 18-hole playoff, both Vardon and Ray cracked under the pressure. But Ouimet was cool as he sank a four-foot putt on the 18th green to win the championship. News of Ouimet's stunning upset made front page headlines from coast to coast, helping to launch the sport toward a day when millions of Americans would play it.

★ ★ ★

During one recent racing season, jockeys at Gulf Stream Park in Florida complained that the finish line was difficult to see as they came hurtling toward it on the back of a horse. Officials at the track mounted a big red disc atop the pole that marked the line, and within the disc in white letters they painted the words "THE END."

★ ★ ★

The shortest baseball player in major-league history was a midget 43 inches in height. His name was Eddie Gaedel and he played for the St. Louis Browns in a game against the Detroit Tigers on August 19, 1951.

In his only trip to the plate, Gaedel walked on four pitches. He was immediately replaced by a pinch runner. The next day, the American League president, claiming that baseball was being subjected to ridicule, banned Gaedel from further participation in the game. Besides his height (or lack of it), Gaedel was distinctive for the number he wore — ⅛.

Bobby Orr's value to the Boston Bruins of the National Hockey League during the late 1960's and early 1970's can't be underestimated. A quick glance at the record book is proof of that. Orr established the scoring record for defensemen in the 1974-75 season, when he registered 46 goals. In addition, Orr, with the 37 goals that he scored in 1970-71 and 1971-72, holds the No. 2 and No. 3 slots on the list of

Bobby Orr

most goals by a defenseman for a season, and he also ranks fourth, fifth, sixth, and tenth on the list.

But Orr was more than merely a scoring machine. He also holds the NHL record for most assists by a defenseman — 102, a mark he set in 1970-71. And his 90 assists in 1973-74 and his 89 assists in 1974-75 earned him second and third position on *that* list.

★ ★ ★

When the University of Pittsburgh's Tony Dorsett won the Heisman Trophy in 1976 as college football's outstanding player, it marked the 27th consecutive year that the award had gone to either a running back (as in Dorsett's case) or a quarterback. Leon Hart, a Notre Dame end, the Heisman winner in 1949, was the last player not a backfield man to be awarded the trophy.

★ ★ ★

Jesse Owens is the only athlete to set six world records in one day. On May 25, 1935, at Evanston, Illinois, Owens ran the 100-yard dash in 9.4 seconds; long-jumped 26 feet, 8¼ inches; ran the 200-yard dash in 20.3 seconds; and ran the 22-yard low hurdles in 22.6 seconds. The two 220-yard events were also certified as 200-meter records.

★ ★ ★

Three football teams representing high schools in San Antonio, Texas, recently held a pancake-eating contest for charity, with the winner to be decided on the basis of which team would gain the most weight. MacArthur High triumphed, gaining an average of 5.5 pounds per man, a total of 110.25 pounds. The outstanding performer of the day was Eddie Lee, a tackle for Alamo Heights High School. Eddie ate 50 pancakes and saw his weight go from 202 to 222 pounds.

★ ★ ★

Major Walter C. Wingfield, a British Army officer, invented the game of tennis, introducing it at a lawn party in Wales in 1873. One of the major's guests that afternoon became enthusiastic about the game, and when he left for Bermuda a few weeks later, he took a supply of balls and rackets with him. Early the next year, Mary Ewing Outerbridge of Staten Island arrived in Bermuda for a vacation, and happened to see tennis being played. She became so fascinated with the sport that she learned the rules and purchased some equipment to take back to the United States. The Outerbridge family held a membership in the Staten Island Cricket and Baseball Club, and Miss Outerbridge was given permission to lay out a tennis court there.

Staten Island women were quick to take to

the sport, but men held back. The constant cry of "love," a scoring term meaning "zero," made the sport seem unmanly to many males. The sport eventually became popular among men, of course, but only after they overcame their masculine prejudices.

The first baseball pitcher to curve a ball was William Arthur (Candy) Cummings, who introduced the pitch in 1866. From Ware, Massachusetts, Cummings pitched for the Excelsior Junior Nine of Brooklyn, New York.

When a quarterback is able to compile 3,000 or more yards with his passes during a season, it's considered a notable achievement. Some quarterbacks never do it, and during the season of 1976, only Bert Jones of the Baltimore Colts did. Jones totaled 3,104 yards with his passes. The all-time record for passing yards gained in a season is held by Joe Namath. In 1967, Namath, then with the New York Jets, rolled up 4,007 with his passes, a spectacular figure.

The first auto race of major importance was held in 1894 over a course laid out from Paris to Rouen, and was won by a steam-powered vehicle that attained a speed of 11 miles per hour. A year later a round-trip race between Paris and Bordeaux produced the speed of 15 miles per hour.

★ ★ ★

It costs about $1.80 a mile to move a basketball team from one city to another. With a baseball team, the cost is $4.50 a mile. Football is even more expensive. Transporting all those players and coaches costs about $7.50 a mile.

★ ★ ★

According to a survey conducted by the A.C. Nielsen Company during the mid-1970's, swimming is the most popular sport in the United States. But the older a person is, the less likely he or she is to swim. The survey found that 80 percent of boys and girls ages 12 to 17 went swimming "from time to time," but less than 50 percent of adult men and women did.

The same was true of ice skating. While popular with young children and teenagers, ice skating had relatively few adult participants.

Here is a list of the most popular participant sports among boys and girls:

Ages 12-17	Under 12
1. Swimming	1. Swimming

2. Bicycling	2. Bicycling
3. Fishing	3. Camping
4. Camping	4. Fishing
5. Basketball	5. Ice Skating
6. Softball	6. Softball
7. Table Tennis	7. Boating
8. Ice Skating	8. Baseball
9. Bowling	9. Table Tennis
10. Pool and Billiards	10. Basketball

★ ★ ★

When Walter Scott of Shamokin, Pennsylvania, tells friends he once bowled a game in which he had 10 strikes, they figure he racked up a score of 270 or 280 or thereabouts. No such luck. Scott, who rolled his 10-strike game in 1966, ended up with a modest 214, the lowest 10-strike game in bowling history. He missed the pins completely with one ball, and got counts of only 2 pins and 3 pins with two other balls. His score sheet looked like this:

X X X 3-0 X X X 7-2 X XXX

★ ★ ★

A horse's snort, whinnies, and neighs may not mean much to the average person, but to Henry Blake, a 46-year-old farmer in Wales, they're pieces of conversation. In his book *Talking With Horses*, Blake presents 47 messages that horses use in expressing themselves. For example, Blake says that when a horse rubs you with his nose or catches your shirt in his mouth and tugs it, he is saying, "I like you" or "I love you." Horses have 30 ways of expressing affection, according to Blake, while humans have only 25.

One of the most unusual basketball games on record took place in 1976 in Spartanburg County, South Carolina, between women's teams from Mabry Junior High School and D.R. Hill Junior High. The D.R. Hill team was unstoppable during the first half, building up a 26-0 lead. Then it was Mabry's turn. In the second half, Mabry scored 28 consecutive points and D.R. Hill didn't score any. Final score: Mabry, 28; D.R. Hill, 26.

In the 1932 Olympic Games in Los Angeles, America's Mildred (Babe) Didrikson won gold medals in the javelin throw and the 80-meter hurdles, thus becoming the first female double-winner in Olympic history. The same year, Lillian Copeland of the United States took the gold medal in the discus throw. Never once in the years that have followed have America's female athletes been victorious in any one of these three events.

The 1920's are often hailed as The Golden

Age of Sport. Baseball had Babe Ruth; football, Red Grange; boxing, Jack Dempsey; and tennis, Bill Tilden. One other glittering sports star of the time is often overlooked — Strangler Lewis, the heavyweight wrestling champion of the world. His real name was Robert Fredericks. When he was 19 years old, he quit playing semipro baseball and began to wrestle professionally. All he knew about the sport was what he had learned from a 50-cent mail-order instruction book written by a man named Evan Lewis. In tribute to Lewis, he took his name, calling himself Ed Lewis. But when he perfected a lethal headlock and used it to win matches, he became known as Strangler Lewis. He took on all contenders in a record total of 6,200 bouts and is said to have amassed more than five million dollars in ring earnings.

During the season of 1973, the Philadelphia Atoms of the North American Soccer League established themselves as the most tenacious defensive team in league history. In 19 games, the Atoms permitted only 14 goals, an average of .74 goals per game. Both figures are all-time NASL records.

When in 1950, the Associated Press polled

393 sports experts to determine the greatest sports upset in the first half of the 20th century, more of them voted for the Boston Braves' four-straight-game World Series victory over the Philadelphia Athletics in 1914 than any other event.

On July 9, 1914, the Braves languished in last place in the National League, 11½ games behind the league-leading New York Giants. Then the team began to climb in the standings. On July 15, the Braves were in fifth place. On July 25, they were second. On August 2, they reached first place, where they stayed. The Braves clinched the pennant in September, the first in the team's history, and kept their magic touch through the World Series. "A ball club which started the season as a joke reached the *perch de luxe* in baseball in a blaze of glory," said *The New York Times*.

★ ★ ★

Salaries in professional basketball average a bit more or less than $100,000 a year. Yet officials of World Team Tennis claim that their players are higher paid than those in basketball. This is how they figure: The average WTT player earns $46,000 a year. But the season lasts only thirteen weeks, meaning that each player earns an average of $3,538 a week. Multiply that by 52 weeks and you get an annual average income of $184,000 for each WTT performer.

★ ★ ★

America's Gertrude Ederle became the first woman to succeed in swimming the English Channel when, on August 6, 1926, she made the crossing from Cap Gris Nez, France, to Dover, England, in the record time of 14 hours, 39 minutes. Florence Chadwick, also an American, became the first woman to swim the Channel from England to France when, on September 11, 1951, she made the crossing in 16 hours, 19 minutes. She repeated the feat on September 4, 1953, and again on October 12, 1955.

★ ★ ★

The speed of a hockey puck, when struck by Gordie Howe of the Houston Aeros, was measured at 118.3 miles per hour.

★ ★ ★

According to the *Guinness Book of World Records*, the record for consecutive basketball free throws by a professional is 499, by Barney Levitt. The highest total by an amateur is 200. But both records were eclipsed in December, 1975, when Hal Cohen, a 6-foot-1 senior guard at Canton, New York, High School, told to practice free throws by his coach, got a string going and couldn't stop. As the gym filled with spectators, Cohen kept shooting. He reached 200 in a row, then 250, then 300. At 400 his coach began to worry that he might be developing blisters, but Cohen assured him he wasn't. At 500, the coach wanted to know if Cohen was getting tired. "No," said Cohen, and kept firing. Finally, an hour and a half after he had begun, Cohen put up a shot that glanced off the front of the rim. By that time he had shattered every record, having completed 575 consecutive free throws.

★ ★ ★

The modern record for strikeouts in a season is 383, set by Nolan Ryan of the California Angels in 1973. But back in the season of 1886, Baltimore's Matt Kilroy struck out 505 batters. What was Kilroy's "secret"? He had none, really. What he did have was a shorter distance to pitch. The pitching rubber was only 50 feet from the plate in Kilroy's day, as compared to 60 feet, 6 inches, the distance that Ryan pitched.

★ ★ ★

R.C. Owens, who joined the San Francisco 49ers as a wide receiver in 1958, had been a splendid basketball player and high jumper in college. One season he had averaged 27.7 rebounds per game, and he had high-jumped seven feet. One day Owens asked San Francisco coach Red Hickey to let him try to block opponent's kicks on field-goal attempts. The goalpost crossbar is 10 feet above the ground.

Sometimes the ball barely clears it. Owens knew that in such cases he could bat the ball away. But Hickey refused to let Owens try his scheme.

After Owens was traded to the Baltimore Colts, he approached coach Weeb Ewbank with his idea. Ewbank said he would give him a chance. The Colts were playing the Redskins. When Bob Khayat of the Redskins got set to try a field goal from the Baltimore 40-yard line, Owens took up a position under the crossbar. Khayat kicked and the ball arched high into the sky, and then began to descend toward the bar. Owens crouched down. As the ball neared the bar, Owens sprang into the air. His hand made contact with the ball and he smacked it away. With his blocked shot, R.C. Owens gained lasting fame as pro football's first goaltender.

Even though the pitcher in softball must throw underhand, he or she can still manage to rocket the ball toward the plate at speeds of about 100 miles an hour. The softball pitcher is also aided by the fact that the rubber is only 45 feet from the plate (as opposed to baseball's 60½ feet). Softball pitchers have been capable of incredible records as a result. For example, Clarence (Buck) Miller, a member of the Softball Hall of Fame, had 96 no-hit games to his credit. The career record for no-hit games in baseball is shared by Sandy Koufax and

Nolan Ryan, each of whom has four. Betty Grayson, another member of the Softball Hall of Fame, once recorded 115 consecutive scoreless innings, the equivalent of about 16 games. She had a fitting nickname — Bullet Betty.

★ ★ ★

Many experts believe that exercise is more important than the nature of one's diet in becoming fit and maintaining fitness. In working off calories, the tennis player, naturally, has the edge over the individual who prefers relaxing on the couch with a good book. The figures below show how many calories can be burned up in one minute for each of the activities listed:

Bicycling	8.2 calories
Reclining	1.3 calories
Running	19.4 calories
Swimming	11.2 calories
Walking	5.2 calories (at 3½ mph)

★ ★ ★

In 1895, the U.S. Golf Association issued an edict saying that a regulation putter had to be used whenever a golfer was attempting to putt. The ruling stemmed from the action of a competitor in the U.S. Amateur Championship at Newport, Rhode Island, that year, who attempted to sink a putt with a billiard cue.

★ ★ ★

How many times did Hank Aaron hit 50 or more home runs in a season? He never did. Aaron's highest season home-run total was 47, the number he hit in 1971.

Only 11 players have hit 50 or more home runs in a season. Babe Ruth did it four times. Willie Mays and Ralph Kiner did it twice.

★ ★ ★

France's Jose Meiffret achieved the highest speed ever on a bicycle — 127.243 miles per hour — on July 19, 1962, at Freiburg, West Germany.

★ ★ ★

Each game in the National Basketball Association consists of four 12-minute quarters, a total of 48 minutes of playing time. Yet during the season of 1961-62, Wilt Chamberlain, then a member of the Philadelphia Warriors, played an average of 48½ minutes per game. How come? Well, Wilt played virtually every minute of every game that season, plus almost a full hour of overtime minutes.

★ ★ ★

The practice of having the President of the United States toss out a ball to open the baseball season was begun by William How-

Babe Ruth

ard Taft. On April 10, 1910, Taft threw out a baseball before the game between the Washing Senators and Philadelphia Athletics, which was won by Washington, 3-0. Attracted by the President, a crowd of 12,226 turned out for the game, setting an attendance record.

★ ★ ★

In their "pep talks" at halftime, football coaches have used a variety of approaches in an effort to lift the spirits of their players. Take the case of Nebraska coach Dana X. Bible. In a game against Indiana in 1936, Nebraska trailed, 9-0, as the players came off the field at the end of the second quarter. Bible was livid. "You don't have the desire to win," he screamed. "You don't have the courage to fight back.

"The first 11 players who go out that door will start the second half," Bible continued. "The rest will sit on the bench."

The players scrambled for the door. Bible put the first 11 who squirmed through on the field — and they beat Indiana, 14-9.

★ ★ ★

The first formal Olympic Games were staged in 776 B.C., with the Greeks establishing a set of rules for each of the various contests. The Olympics were banned by the Romans in 392 B.C., because Emperor Theodosius decided that they had become a public nuisance.

The Games were revived in 1896, largely through the effort of a young French baron, Pierre de Coubertin. A Harvard freshman named James B. Connolly, who paid his own expenses to Athens, outclassed his rivals in the hop, step, and jump event to become the first gold medal winner in almost 22 centuries.

★ ★ ★

The Chicago Black Hawks of the National Hockey League were shut out a record eight consecutive games during the season of 1928-29. As if to make amends for that period of helplessness, the Black Hawks later established the league's longest non-shutout record. It lasted 228 games and covered a period of close to three years, from March 14, 1970 to February 21, 1973.

★ ★ ★

According to the American League, the Cleveland Indians have the best geographic location of any team in terms of travel time and expense. Cleveland has to travel only about 19,000 miles a year. Atlantic Coast teams — the Baltimore Orioles, New York Yankees, and Boston Red Sox — must travel as much as 30,000 miles in a year. And the Pacific Coast teams — the Oakland A's and California

Angels, etc. — travel the most, from 40,000 to 45,000 miles a year.

★ ★ ★

The first play-by-play radio broadcast of a football game was presented on November 25, 1920, by station WTAW of College Station, Texas. The University of Texas played Texas A & M. The station was operating under an experimental license at the time, and used 5XB as its call letters.

The following year, 1921, the first play-by-play description of a baseball game was aired, when, on August 5, station KDKA in Pittsburgh broadcast an account of a contest between the Pirates and the Philadelphia Phillies.

★ ★ ★

Professional basketball has a continual problem with officiating of games, and baseball officials often ponder what they can do to speed up things. But Obare Asiko, commissioner of the Kenya Football Association, recently confronted a problem much more formidable than any ever faced by American officials. Asiko felt it necessary to warn practicing witch doctors that anyone found guilty of casting spells during soccer games would be subject to criminal prosecution. Local witch doctors had been claiming they could cast spells on opposing players with bird and animal charms. "The practice of witchcraft is unsettling our efforts to clean up soccer," Asiko declared.

★ ★ ★

The biggest spread in a National Basketball Association game occurred during the 1971-72 season when the Los Angeles Lakers defeated the Golden State Warriors, 162-99. The most common point spread in NBA games is two points. In the first 12,968 NBA games played, the two-point spread occurred 949 times. The second most common point spread was four points. It occurred 821 times.

★ ★ ★

Larry Wos, a 46-year-old mathematician from Joliet, Illinois, who has been blind since birth, discovered bowling at the age of 27, and now bowls three times a week. He uses a guide rail to align his approach, and a spotter to tell him which pins, if any, he's left standing. He boasts a 132 average, has a high game of 233, and once held the championship of the American Blind Bowling Association, an organization of more than 2,000 in 30 states.

Wos once took on professional bowler Ernie Schlegel in an exhibition match. Schlegel, who had a 211 average, was blindfolded and used the guide rail to align his approach. He could rarely find the alley. Wos, with four spares and a strike, trounced him, 132-50.

★ ★ ★

On July 18, 1951, at the age of 37, Jersey Joe Walcott was given his fifth and what was generally believed to be his final opportunity to win the heavyweight boxing title. His opponent was champion Ezzard Charles, who had previously twice beaten Walcott. Early in the seventh round, Walcott unleashed a powerful left hook that caught Charles flush on the jaw. He pitched forward, collapsed on the ring floor, and was counted out. Walcott was hailed as the new champion, the oldest fighter in history to win the heavyweight crown.

★ ★ ★

Antonio Abertondo, an Argentinian, was the first swimmer to make a round-trip crossing of the English Channel. He accomplished the feat on September 20 and 21, 1961, covering the distance in 43 hours, 10 minutes. The feat has since been duplicated four times. The fastest double crossing was one of 30 hours, achieved by Jon Erikson on August 14 and 15, 1975.

★ ★ ★

Johnny Bench of the Cincinnati Reds climaxed a brilliant showing in the 1976 World Series by driving in five runs with two homers in the Series-winning fourth game. Bench had a total of eight hits in 15 at-bats for the Series, played with his usual excellence behind the plate, and won the Most Valuable Player award — to no one's surprise.

Bench also accomplished something that had been done only nine times before in World Series history, when he achieved a slugging average in excess of 1.000. It was 1.133 (17 total bases divided by 15 at-bats). Here is a list of the other leading World Series sluggers (based on at least 10 at-bats):

Player, Team	*Year*	*Slugging Average*
Lou Gehrig, New York Yankees	1928	1.727
Babe Ruth, New York Yankees	1928	1.375
Hank Gowdy, Boston Braves	1914	1.273
Charlie Keller, New York Yankees	1939	1.188
Johnny Bench, Cincinnati Reds	1976	1.133
Lou Gehrig, New York Yankees	1932	1.118
John Blanchard, New York Yankees	1961	1.100
Donn Clendenon, New York Mets	1969	1.071
Johnny Mize, New York Yankees	1952	1.067
Babe Ruth, New York Yankees	1923	1.000

Early in 1976, seven-year-old Daniel Tveit of St. Paul, Minnesota, became the youngest winner ever in the 31st annual St. Paul Winter Carnival ice-fishing contest when he hooked and landed a 3-pound 7-ounce Northern pike one hour after the competition began. There were 6,000 other anglers in competition with him.

Lou Gehrig

★ ★ ★

The Olympic Games are meant to stress individual excellence and promote international goodwill. But sometimes these goals are forgotten. In 1936, when the Games were held in Berlin, Adolph Hitler was determined to use them to prove his master-race theories. But his plans were frustrated by Jesse Owens, the star of the American team that year.

Owens, a black man, was an inferior in Hitler's eyes. When Owens won the 100-meter dash, the long jump, and the 200-meter dash, Hitler watched from his special box. Then when Owens stood proudly on the platform to accept his gold medals, Hitler made a point of looking the other way.

The 400-meter relay race was the next event on the program, and Owens sparked the United States team to a victory. Hitler stormed angrily out of his box, unable to watch Owens demonstrate the mythical nature of his theory of Aryan supremacy.

★ ★ ★

In 1875, Charles C. Waite, the first baseman for the National Association's Bostons, became the first baseball player to use a glove. To wear a glove or other protective equipment was considered effeminate in those days; therefore Waite's glove was flesh color so it wouldn't be conspicuous.

★ ★ ★

Hurling, a game in which two teams of 15 men each attempt to put a small horsehide covered ball in one another's net goal using sticks much like field-hockey sticks, is as Irish as the shamrock. It is believed to have been played in Ireland before the arrival of St. Patrick.

When the Gaelic Athletic Association was founded in 1884, and established the rules for hurling, one of its regulations raised some eyebrows. Hurling players and officials were forbidden to play, watch, or otherwise encourage the sports of soccer, rugby, and cricket. These games were considered British games, and Ireland at the time was suffering under British rule.

The Irish won their independence in 1922, when the constitution of the Irish Free State was adopted. But the Gaelic Athletic Association has never changed its regulation concerning soccer, rugby, and cricket, and hurling players and officials are still prohibited from any association with them.

★ ★ ★

Tight end Marv Fleming, who joined the Green Bay Packers in 1963 and was traded to the Miami Dolphins in 1970, won a reputation for being with the right team at the right time. In 1967 and 1968, Fleming went to the Super Bowl with the Packers, and in 1972, 1973, and

1974, he went as a member of the Dolphins. That's five Super Bowl appearances, more than any other pro player.

The records for basketball's longest winning streak during regular season play and the longest playoff winning streak are both held by the Los Angeles Lakers. From the period of November 5, 1971 to January 7, 1972, the Lakers won a record 33 games in a row. And in playoff competition from April 5 to April 19, 1970, the Los Angeles team won seven consecutive times.

As an astronaut-turned-aquanaut, M. Scott Carpenter established records not only in outer space, but on the ocean floor as well. In 1962, as commander of the Mercury-Atlas 7 space mission, Carpenter orbited the earth three times, spending 4 hours, 56 minutes in space, more elapsed time than any other American up to that date. Three years later, aboard Sealab II, Carpenter spent 30 days at a depth of 205 feet in the Pacific Ocean, establishing a world record for an underwater stay.

Up until about 1848, the golf ball was made from a leather cover stuffed with feathers. This was replaced with the gutta percha ball, one made from the rubberlike substance obtained from the latex of certain trees common to Malaysia. In 1900, at the Balmalewan Club in New Zealand, Andrew Todd is said to have driven a "gutty" 428 yards. The rubber core ball in use today dates to 1902.

During the 1928-29 season, goalie George Hainsworth of the Montreal Canadiens established a National Hockey League record by shutting out opponents 22 times. What's amazing about Hainsworth's achievement is that he did it during a season that was a mere 44 games in length.

Joe DiMaggio's hitting streak of 56 consecutive games is considered one of baseball's most amazing performances. The Yankee center fielder began his string on May 15, 1941, and continued through July 16, a two-month period in which he hit at a .408 clip.

A soccer game is invariably a low-scoring contest, and games of such scores as 2-1 or 3-2 are frequent. Fans who watched Toronto play Chicago in a North American Soccer League game in August 27, 1968, must have rubbed

Joe DiMaggio

their eyes in disbelief. A record 12 goals were scored, Toronto winning, 8-4.

★ ★ ★

The biggest bowling center in the world — 180 lanes — is located in Tokyo. The 116-lane Willow Park Lanes in Willow Grove, Pennsylvania, is the biggest bowling center in the United States.

★ ★ ★

High school and college athletes are honored by being awarded a school letter. The first letter in sports history was a "C" — for the University of Chicago. Its use dates to 1906, the year that Amos Alonzo Stagg established the first letterman's club.

★ ★ ★

When the Los Angeles Lakers' Kareem Abdul-Jabbar won the National Basketball Association's Most Valuable Player award in 1977, it marked the fifth time that he had received the award in seven years. Abdul-Jabbar was the overwhelming winner in the voting by 247 NBA players, receiving 159 votes to 29 for Bill Walton, center for the Portland Trail Blazers, the runner-up. Only one other player in NBA history has won the league MVP award five times — Bill Russell, who played 13 seasons for the Boston Celtics.

★ ★ ★

Women were not only barred as competitors in the original Olympic Games in ancient Greece, they were also punished with death for even looking at the events. But women of the time were determined to participate in athletics. Hippodameia of Athens organized the Heraea Games for women runners. Like the Olympiad, the competition was held every four years.

The prejudice against women in sports lasted until fairly recent times. When the modern Olympic Games began in 1896, there were no events for women. In 1900, women were permitted to compete in Olympic tennis and equestrian events, but these were dropped from the schedule four years later. There was women's archery in 1908, and women's swimming in 1912. It wasn't until after World War I, which triggered an increase in women's rights and opportunities in general, that women became accepted as Olympic competitors in a wide range of events.

The youngest major-league baseball player of all time was Joe Nuxhall, a pitcher for the Cincinnati Reds. He was 15 years, 10 months, and 11 days when he joined the team in June, 1944.

A badminton shuttlecock, a small and rounded piece of cork with a crown of feathers, is not meant to be hit over a long distance. But Frank Rugani, in tests performed at San Jose, California, on February 29, 1964, managed to whack a "bird," as it is sometimes called, a distance of 79 feet, 8½ inches, which is believed to be the record.

Goalies for the Quebec Bulldogs during 1919-20 were not noted for their competence. In the 24 games played that season, Bulldog goaltenders saw the puck whiz into the net 177 times, an average of 7.38 times per game, the National League record.

★ ★ ★

Henry Armstrong was the only boxer in history to hold championships in three different weight divisions simultaneously. The 27-year-old Armstrong held the featherweight, lightweight, and welterweight titles from August to December, 1938.

★ ★ ★

Cincinnati entered the National Football League for the first time in 1921 with a team called the Celts. The Cincinnati Celts played eight games and lost all eight, and then dropped out of the league. Cincinnati tried again in 1933, this time with a team known as the Reds. The Reds managed to win three games of the 10 they played, and enjoyed a moment of excitement in the season's finale against the Brooklyn Dodgers when rookie Gil Lefebvre, who was 5-foot-6, returned a punt 98 yards for a touchdown. It was not the distance that Lefebvre covered that caused the excitement. His touchdown represented one-third of the touchdowns scored by the Reds that season. It's a record that still stands: No team has ever registered fewer than three touchdowns in a season.

★ ★ ★

The American League put the designated hitter rule into effect in 1973. It stated that a hitter could be designated to bat for the starting pitcher without the pitcher's status being otherwise affected. Ron Blomberg of the New York Yankees became the first designated hitter in baseball history, and the bat he used was sent to the Baseball Hall of Fame in Cooperstown, New York, to be put on display.

★ ★ ★

"Ageless" was the word often used to describe Stella Walsh, who set almost 100 different track and field records during her long career. She first came to prominence at the Olympic Games in 1932, when, as Stanislawa Walasiewicz, and representing Poland, she won the 100-meter dash. Soon after, she immigrated to the United States and changed her name to Stella Walsh. During the late 1930's and throughout the 1940's, she raced in track events in distances ranging from 60 yards to a mile. She also competed as a broad jumper, high jumper, shot-putter, hurdler, and discus thrower. It is estimated that she took part in more than 1,110 different events.

Beginning in 1950, she won the United States pentathlon championship five consecutive times. In 1962, 30 years after her Olympic triumph, she was still competing against the best athletes of the day. She was then 51 years old.

★ ★ ★

Fifteen-year-old Charlotte (Lottie) Dod of England became the youngest champion in Wimbledon history when she won the women's singles title. She also captured the Wimbledon singles championship in 1888, 1891, 1892, and 1893. Wilfred Badderly holds the distinction of being the youngest male singles champion at Wimbledon. When he won the title in 1891, Badderly's age was 19.

★ ★ ★

In 1976, his final college year, running back Tony Dorsett of the University of Pittsburgh didn't merely make the record book, he rewrote it, setting 18 National Collegiate Athletic Association (NCAA) marks. Dorsett was also a landslide winner in the voting for the Heisman Trophy that year. His most important records were:

- Most yards gained (1976) — 1,948
- Most touchdowns, career (tie with Glenn Davis — 59)
- Most points, career — 356
- Most yards gained, career — 6,082
- Most rushes, career — 1,074

★ ★ ★

Monte Cross, an outfielder with the Philadelphia A's during the early 1900's, compiled the lowest batting average in major-league history in 1904. Playing in 153 games and batting 503 times, Cross hit — if that is the word — .182.

★ ★ ★

Mac Wilkins of the United States won the discus event in the 1976 Olympic Games with a throw of 221 feet, 5 inches. When Al Oerter won the discus throw in 1956, his heave measured 184 feet, 10 inches. It's like that in virtually all track and field sports. Athletes keep getting better and better. A glaring exception is the 16-pound hammer throw. America's Harold Connolly won the event in the 1956 Olympics with a throw of 207 feet, 3 inches, and in 1960 Connolly threw the hammer 230 feet (not in Olympic competition, however). But in the U.S. Olympic Trials in 1976, the best throw was a mere 222 feet, 7 inches, more than six feet shorter than the distance Connolly used to achieve. A throw of 226 feet, 7 inches was necessary to qualify for Olympic competition, so no American qualified. What's happened? Why are Americans seemingly going backwards in this event? "It's the coaching," Connolly says. "Most hammer throwers don't have a coach, and they don't know what to do. They're just stumbling around."

★ ★ ★

According to the *National Police Gazette*, in an issue dated September 20, 1890, the first women's baseball team was known as the Young Ladies' Baseball Team No. 1. The team toured the country during the season of 1890, playing men's teams. The players included: May Howard, pitcher; Nellie Williams, catcher; Kittie Grant, first base; Angie Parker, second base; Edith Mayres, third base; Effie Earl, shortstop; Alice Lee, left field; Rose Mitchell, right field; and Annie Grant, center field.

★ ★ ★

Egypt's Abla Khairi became the youngest person to swim the English Channel, when, on August 18, 1974, he made the crossing from Cap Gris Nez in France to Dover, England, in the time of 12 hours, 30 minutes. He was 13 years old at the time.

★ ★ ★

What is billed as the "toughest track event in the United States" is not a 10,000-meter run in the wintertime nor a marathon over hilly terrain. It's the National 100-Mile Walking Championship. Contestants must finish the race within 24 hours, which means that a pace of 14 minutes per mile must be maintained, allowing 40 minutes for restroom stops and clothing changes. In the 10th renewal of the event, held in Columbia, Missouri, late in 1976, 30 walkers entered the event, and only seven finished. Twenty-five-year-old Augie Hirt, who came across the finish line with his eyes half closed, his feet dragging, won the race in 19 hours, 55 minutes, 16 seconds.

In Cincinnati on October 12, 1910, Sheldon Lejeunne threw a baseball a distance of 426 feet, 9½ inches. It still stands as the longest throw ever recorded.

Goaltender Sam LoPresti of the Chicago Black Hawks attained an unenviable distinction in a game against the Boston Bruins on March 4, 1941. LoPresti was bombarded by a record 83 shots, yet the Bruins just managed to win, 3-2.

It's anyone's guess how long the people of Hawaii have been surfing. But an entry in the log of Lieutenant James King of His Majesty's Navy told of the "altogether astonishing" sight of natives atop flat boards skimming along the crests of tall Hawaiian waves. The entry was written in 1779.

★ ★ ★

When the Cleveland Browns of the late 1950's and early 1960's wanted a touchdown, they gave the ball to Jim Brown. The strategy usually worked. In his nine seasons with the Cleveland team, Brown scored a record 126 touchdowns. Other players threatened Brown's mark, but they all retired before reaching it. Among active players, no one is within hailing distance of him. Here is a list of pro football's top ten touchdown scorers:

Player	*Seasons*	*Total Touchdowns*
Jim Brown	9	126
Lenny Moore	12	113
Don Hutson	11	105
Jim Taylor	10	93
Bobby Mitchell	11	91
Leroy Kelly	10	90
Charley Taylor	12	90
Don Maynard	15	88
Lance Alworth	11	87
Tommy McDonald	12	85

★ ★ ★

How far can a professional player drive a golf ball? That question isn't difficult to answer today. Through the years, constantly improving manufacturing techniques enabled equipment companies to produce golf balls that traveled farther and farther, despite standards of weight, size, and velocity that had been set down by the United States Golf Association. But in 1976, the U.S.G.A. announced a new rule that mandated that a ball, as tested on an outdoor range, must not roll or carry more than 280 yards. The regulation permits an eight percent variation from the standard, meaning the ball can travel a maximum distance of 302.4 yards. So *that's* how far a professional player can drive a golf ball.

★ ★ ★

During the National Basketball Association's 1976-77 season, Elvin Hayes of the Washington Bullets led all players in the amount of playing time. He appeared in every one of the Bullets' 82 regular season games, averaging 41 minutes per game.

But two of Hayes' teammates — Tom Henderson and Leon Gray — appeared in more games than Hayes did. Considering that Hayes appeared in *every* game, how could that be possible? In Henderson's case, here's what happened: He played 46 games for the Atlanta Hawks, and then he was traded to Washington, which had played five fewer games than the Hawks at the time. Henderson appeared in 41 games of the Bullets' remaining games, a total of 87 games for the season.

Gray appeared in 83 games — 25 with the Seattle Supersonics before he was traded to the Bullets; he then played 58 games for the Washington team.

★ ★ ★

During the mid-19th century, when boxing matches were conducted under the London Prize Ring Rules, bare knuckles were used, and a round ended when a fighter was knocked down or wrestled to the ground. The Marquis of Queensbury Rules, devised by John Sholto Douglas in 1867, were more humane. Wrestling or hugging were not allowed; each round lasted three minutes with a one-minute rest in between rounds; a man knocked to the canvas had to get up before the count of 10; and boxing gloves had to be worn. With only minor variations, the rules are in use today in every part of the world where boxing is to be found

★ ★ ★

In the years after he joined the New York Jets in 1969, Steve O'Neal was seldom considered more than a journeyman punter. But one September afternoon during his rookie season in a game against the Denver Broncos, O'Neal booted the longest punt in football history, a stunning 98-yarder. It was generally agreed that where the game happened to be played was a factor — in the rarefied air of Denver.

★ ★ ★

Capturing the triple crown in baseball, that is, winning the batting, home run, and runs-batted-in titles in one season, is a rare achievement. Only nine players have done it, and none since Carl Yastrzemski of the Boston Red Sox in 1967. The others include:

Frank Robinson, Baltimore Orioles, 1966
Mickey Mantle, New York Yankees, 1956
Ted Williams, Boston Red Sox, 1942, 1947
Joe Medwick, St. Louis Cardinals, 1937
Lou Gehrig, New York Yankees, 1934
Chuck Klein, Philadelphia Phillies, 1933
Jimmy Foxx, Philadelphia A's, 1933
Rogers Hornsby, St. Louis Cardinals, 1922, 1925

Ted Williams

★ ★ ★

Twenty-two-year-old Danny Seemiller of Carrick, Pennsylvania, a Pittsburgh suburb, the No. 1 table-tennis player in the United States since 1973, began playing the game when he was 12, and he won the U.S. Junior Championship while still in high school. His ambition is to win the world title. In 1976, Seemiller accomplished something no other American had achieved in 15 years — a world ranking. He was classified as the 29th best player in the world.

★ ★ ★

The earliest recorded parachute jump in the United States took place in 1838, when balloonist John Wise made a 13,000 foot descent using an inverted chute. The importance of parachute jumping was demonstrated during World War I, when chutists were landed behind enemy lines for espionage purposes.

In 1914, a woman, Tiny Broadwick, made the first freefall jump. In freefall, the chutist falls for a certain amount of time before opening the chute. Miss Broadwick's daring jump paved the way for other freefall attempts, which eventually led to the development of sport parachuting.

★ ★ ★

On November 24, 1949, in a game against the

Chicago Bears, Bob Smith of the Detroit Lions intercepted a pass in his own end zone, and raced the length of the field for a touchdown. The game's statistician credited Smith with a 102-yard interception return, the longest in football history. The feat was duplicated by Erich Barnes of the New York Giants against the Dallas Cowboys in 1961.

★ ★ ★

Were a player in the National Hockey League to ever average a goal a game during a season, it would be considered superlative. Among modern players, Phil Esposito came closest to achieving that feat. During 1970-71, Esposito, a member of the Boston Bruins at the time, scored 76 goals in 78 games, a .97 goal-per-game average.

Oldtime players had much higher averages. During the 1917-18 season, Joe Malone of the Montreal Canadiens scored 44 goals in 20 games, a stunning 2.20 goals-per-game average. The career record in this regard is held by Cy Denneny, who played 12 seasons with the Ottawa Senators and the Boston Bruins. The Senators' scoring leader in 1917-18, 1920-21, 1921-22, 1923-24, and 1924-25, Denneny scored 250 goals in 326 games, a .767 average.

★ ★ ★

In 1956, when Floyd Patterson was 21 years old, he stunned the boxing world by knocking out Archie Moore to win the heavyweight championship of the world, becoming the youngest prizefighter to ever gain the heavyweight title. Four years later, after having lost the title to Sweden's Ingemar Johansson, Patterson made history again when he defeated Johansson in a rematch, thus becoming the first heavyweight fighter in history to regain his title.

The Big Four tennis tournaments are Wimbledon, the U.S. Open, and the French and Australian Opens. Roy Emerson, player-coach of the Boston Lobsters of World Team Tennis, has won 12 Big Four singles championships, more than any other player in tennis history.

While Babe Ruth's season home-run record has been eclipsed (by Roger Maris) and his lifetime mark surpassed (by Hank Aaron), there is one achievement of his that is not in any danger of being equaled, and that is the record he holds for home-run frequency. Ruth struck his 714 lifetime home run in 8,399 times at bat, which gives him an average of one home run for each 11.76 official trips to the plate (a figure you get by dividing the times at bat by the total home runs). Hank Aaron averaged a home run in each 16.37 times at bat (12,364 at bats; 755 home runs). Here is a list of the leading home-run hitters based on home-run frequency:

Player, Team	At Bats Per Home Run
1. Babe Ruth, New York Yankees	11.76
2. Ralph Kiner, Pittsburgh Pirates	14.11
3. Harmon Killebrew, Minnesota Twins	14.22
4. Willie McCovey, San Francisco Giants	14.58
5. Ted Williams, Boston Red Sox	14.79
6. Mickey Mantle, New York Yankees	15.12
7. Jimmy Foxx, Boston Red Sox	15.23
8. Hank Greenberg, Detroit Tigers	15.69
9. Lou Gehrig, New York Yankees	16.23
10. Hank Aaron, Milwaukee Brewers	16.37

When Bill Russell, the All-Pro center for the Boston Celtics, learned that his chief rival, Wilt Chamberlain, had signed a contract for $100,000 for the 1965-66 pro basketball season, he fumed. Russell, who had been offered $70,000 for the season, had not the slightest doubt that he was the best player in the game, and he felt that he should be paid accordingly. He demanded a salary that was higher than Chamberlain's, the highest paid player in the game at the time. Eventually, the Celtics obliged, and prepared a contract for Russell that assured that he would be paid more than Chamberlain. Russell happily signed for $100,001.

★ ★ ★

In September, 1976, 18-year-old Keith Brown of Baltimore became the first athlete in history to win three gold medals in the National Junior Olympics. He excelled in the sprint events, winning at 100 yards (in 9.73 seconds), 200 yards (21.48 seconds), and 440 yards (47.05 seconds).

★ ★ ★

It's considered a splendid feat when a pitcher wins 20 or more games in a season. Win 30 or more games and you're a superstar. How, then, does one rate Detroit's Charlie A. Baldwin, who won 42 games in 1886? And what about Charles "Old Hoss" Radbourne, who, pitching for Providence in 1884, won 60 games?

★ ★ ★

Joe Louis reigned for a longer period than any other heavyweight champion — 11 years, 8 months, and 9 days. He won the championship by knocking out James J. Braddock in the eighth round of their bout in Chicago on June 22, 1937, and he remained as champion until he retired on March 1, 1949. During that period, Louis defended his title 25 times.

★ ★ ★

Around 1825, the world's billiards champion, an Englishman named Jack Carr, discovered that by striking the cue ball to the right or left, or high or low, he could cause it to travel in an unorthodox manner. Today it is a universal practice, and is referred to as "putting English" on the ball.

Basketball is one of a small handful of American sports to be consciously thought up by an individual. The game was "invented" by Dr. James A. Naismith, an instructor at the Young Men's Christian Association Training School in Springfield, Massachusetts, in the winter of 1890-91. Dr. Naismith was seeking an activity for his students, who were bored with calisthenics and other indoor sports activities of the day. The first basketball game was played on January 20, 1891.

What is usually regarded as baseball's most tenacious pitching duel took place on May 2, 1917, at Wrigley Field in Chicago, the Cubs vs. the Cincinnati Reds. Both Jim Vaughn of the Cubs and Fred Toney of the Reds pitched a full nine innings without either man allowing a hit, the only double no-hitter in major league annals. In the top half of the 10th inning, Vaughn relinquished the game's first hit, and the man later scored on an error. When Toney set the Cubs down without a hit in the bottom of the 10th, he and the Reds were the winners, 1-0.

★ ★ ★

Only once in National Hockey League history has a team failed to average at least one goal per game. It happened during the 1928-29 season, when the Chicago Black Hawks scored 33 goals in 44 games, a .75 goal-per-game average.

★ ★ ★

Spain is to bullfighting what Hawaii is to surfing. There are about 650 bullfights a year in Spain. Mexico is the scene of about 250. Bullfighting is also popular in Colombia, Venezuela, Peru, Ecuador, France, and Portugal.

★ ★ ★

Fanny Blankers-Koen, a Dutch housewife and the mother of two children, won recognition as one of the greatest track athletes of all time at the 1948 Olympic Games. Although the "Marvelous Mama," as she was nicknamed, held the world's record in the high jump and broad jump, she decided not to enter these events at the Olympics, but made up her mind to concentrate on running instead. She won the 100-meter dash in 11.9 seconds, the 200-meter dash in 24.4 seconds, and the 80-meter hurdles in 11.2 seconds, a record. She thus became the first female triple winner in Olympic history.

But Mrs. Blankers-Koen was not finished. She anchored the Dutch team to a victory in the 200-meter relay, and became the first woman to win four gold medals in one edition of the Olympic Games.

Eddie Rommel, who became an umpire in the American League in 1938, holds the distinction of being the first umpire to wear eyeglasses. He donned them for a game between the New York Yankees and Washington Senators on April 18, 1956.

The Notre Dame football team of 1924 was one of the most glamorous in history, largely because of its much publicized backfield, known as the Four Horsemen. The team went through the season undefeated, and then beat Stanford in the Rose Bowl at Pasadena, California, on New Year's Day, 1925.

It's not likely that the Four Horsemen would have been successful as modern college backs. Elmer Layden, the fullback, weighed 162 pounds, as did halfback Don Miller. Jim Crowley, the other halfback, weighed 164 pounds, and quarterback Harry Stuhldreher, a mere 154 pounds. Since today's college backs weigh from 170 to 190 pounds, the Four Horsemen might have difficulty making the starting team.

★ ★ ★

The Miami Dolphins of 1972 were perhaps the most devastating team in pro-football history. Powered by the bone-crunching running of Larry Csonka and Jim Kiick, the Dolphins won every game in the regular season; whipped the Cleveland Browns, 14-7, in the divisional playoff; beat the Pittsburgh Steelers, 21-17, to capture the championship of the American Conference; and then trimmed the Washington Redskins, 14-7, in the Super Bowl. That gave the Dolphins a 17-0 record for the season, the most successful in pro-football history.

Larry Csonka

★ ★ ★

In 1938, Johnny Vander Meer, a 23-year-old left-handed pitcher with the Cincinnati Reds, achieved lasting fame by pitching no-hit, no-run games back-to-back. On June 11, Vander Meer hurled the Reds to a 3-0 win over the Boston Bees. Just four days later, Vander Meer blanked the Brooklyn Dodgers, 6-0, before a capacity crowd at Ebbets Field. The fact that it was the first night baseball game at Ebbets Field added to the drama.

★ ★ ★

In November, 1975, Pat Bundy, a senior at Cathedral Preparatory High School in Erie, Pennsylvania, became the first person to swim Lake Erie. He covered the 31 miles from Long Point, Canada, to Presque Isle, Pennsylvania, in 25 hours, 52 minutes.

★ ★ ★

Cross-country racing, a popular form of competitive running in virtually every American high school and college, is one of the most demanding of all sports. Runners can cover up to 25 miles in a day in preparation for a race. But it takes more than stamina to be successful. You also have to have a sense ot timing that enables you to properly pace yourself.

Many cross-country champions have distinguished themselves in long-distance events.

These include Steve Prefontaine, who established the American records for 10,000 meters (27 minutes, 43.6 seconds), the six-mile run (26 minutes, 51.4 seconds), and the three-mile run (12 minutes, 51.4 seconds) in 1974; and Frank Shorter, the marathon winner in the 1972 Olympic Games.

★ ★ ★

Golfing's longest hole is the 17th hole at North Carolina's Black Mountain Golf Club. It measures 745 yards and is rated a par 6.

★ ★ ★

There are approximately 40,000 sky divers in the United States and they make more than one and a half million jumps annually. There are more than 500 parachute clubs and approximately 50 commercial parachute centers.

Sport parachutists compete on the basis of both style and accuracy. Before opening the chute, the jumper performs turns, loops, rolls and other maneuvers, and is graded on his performance, with points being deducted for faults. Once the routine is completed and the chute opened, the landing spot — a small target centered in a cross — is crucial. Many sky divers have the ability to score direct hits on the target following jumps of a mile or more.

★ ★ ★

The Federation Internationale de Football (F.I.F.A.), the international governing body of soccer, was founded in Paris on May 21, 1904, and introduced competition for the World Cup in 1930. Brazil, with its Cup victory in 1970, became the only country in the world to win the competition three times. Brazil had previously won in 1958 and 1962.

★ ★ ★

Hank Aaron once named Jim Rice, a rookie with the Boston Red Sox in 1975, as one player who might surpass his home-run total. Aaron admired Rice for his strength. "He's built like a bull," said Aaron. And he felt that the Red Sox slugger would be helped by the short fences at Fenway Park. It will be another decade or so, however, before Rice accumulates enough home runs to be regarded as a serious challenger.

But there is one player whose home-run total has already exceeded Aaron's. He plays for the Yomiuri Giants of Japan, and has been averaging 40 or so home runs a season since the mid-1950's. His name is Sadshuro Oh. He is known as the Babe Ruth of Japan. Not only has Oh hit more home runs than Aaron, he seems certain to become the first 800-plus home-run hitter in baseball history.

★ ★ ★

Belgium's Leon Vanderstuyft achieved the greatest distance traveled on a bicycle in one hour — 76 miles, 604 yards — on September 30, 1928, on the Montlhery Motor Circuit in France.

★ ★ ★

On October 25, 1929, Allie Brandt of Lockport, New York, bowled games of 297, 289, and 300 for an 886 series, the highest three-game series in official league competition in bowling history. In the decades since, Brandt's record has been threatened many times, most recently by John Wilcox, Jr., of Williamsport, Pennsylvania, who rolled an 885 series in 1972, but no one has managed to equal it.

Leon Bentley of Lorain, Ohio, bowled three consecutive 300 games on March 26, 1931, giving him a 900 series. And at least two other bowlers have done the same thing. But these games were not rolled in sanctioned league play, and hence are not deemed official by the American Bowling Congress.

★ ★ ★

The first instance of a player being paid to play football occurred on November 12, 1892, when William (Pudge) Heffelfinger, said to be the greatest Yale lineman of all time, was given $500 by the Allegheny Athletic Association to join the team for a game against the

Pittsburgh Athletic Club. The money was well spent, for Heffelfinger turned a fumble he recovered into a touchdown, and Allegheny won, 4-0. (A touchdown was worth only two points in those days.)

★ ★ ★

The ability to steal bases *and* hit home runs is a rare one. Up until 1977, there were only five players in major-league history who accumulated as many as 30 stolen bases and 30 home runs in one season. Willie Mays, during his seasons with the Giants, did it twice. Bobby Bonds of the Texas Rangers is the all-time leader, having done it three times. Here is a list of the players who have had 30 or more stolen bases and hit 30 or more home runs in one season:

Player	*Year*	*Stolen Bases*	*Home Runs*
Ken Williams	1922	37	39
Willie Mays	1956	40	36
Willie Mays	1957	38	35
Hank Aaron	1963	31	44
Bobby Bonds	1969	45	32
Tommy Harper	1970	38	31
Bobby Bonds	1973	43	39
Bobby Bonds	1975	32	30

★ ★ ★

On August 19, 1971, Matt Throne of Millbrae, California, became the youngest bowler in the

Willie Mays

history of the sport to roll a perfect game in sanctioned league competition. Matt was 12 years old at the time.

★ ★ ★

When the American Basketball Association set up shop in 1967, it introduced the three-point field goal. For any basket from beyond 25 feet, a team was awarded three points. Some ABA players became surprisingly accurate in hitting shots of this type. During the 1968-69 season, Louis Dampier of the Kentucky Colonels scored a record 199 three-point field goals. In the season of 1974-75, Billy Shepherd of the Memphis Sounds was successful on a record 42 percent of his three-point field-goal tries (60 field goals in 143 attempts).

★ ★ ★

Winning gold medals in gymnastics for excellence on the balance beam, the uneven parallel bars, and in all-around competition at the Olympic Games in Montreal in 1976, 14-year-old Nadia Comaneci (ko-mah-NEECH), the daughter of a Romanian automobile mechanic, enchanted tens of thousands of spectators and the hundreds of millions who watched on television. "The Princess of the Games" she was called. Nadia wasn't merely excellent; she was perfect. For performances on the balance beam and uneven bars, she earned seven perfect 10 scores. Never before had even one 10 been registered in Olympic competition.

Nadia Comaneci

★ ★ ★

In 1863, James Plimpton designed the first practical four-wheeled skate, and three years later he opened the first public roller rink in Newport, Rhode Island. With the introduction of the ball-bearing skate in 1884, roller skating grew by leaps and bounds. Today there are approximately 5,000 roller-skating rinks in the United States. The efficiency of the skate itself has developed to such a degree that a roller skater can speed a distance of 400 meters within a few seconds of the time required by an ice skater.

★ ★ ★

In football, when a punt-return man thrusts a hand over his head to signal a fair catch, the opposing team is not permitted to tackle him, while he himself is not permitted to run with the ball. Whenever Emlen Tunnell of the New York Giants called for a fair catch during his rookie year of 1948, the fans booed him for what they believed to be his lack of courage. Tunnell hated being booed. He made up his mind that he would never field a punt without trying to advance it. Tunnell has to get high marks for his perseverance. By the time he retired in 1961, he had established the all-time record for punt returns (258), and once, against the New York Yanks in 1950, Tunnell returned a record eight punts in a single game.

★ ★ ★

During 1977, Lou Brock of the St. Louis Cardinals won recognition as baseball's greatest thief, breaking Ty Cobb's career record for the most stolen bases (892). In 1974, Brock, with 118 steals, set the season record for stolen bases. And for 12 consecutive seasons beginning in 1965, Brock stole 50 or more bases, another record. But there is one stolen base record that still belongs to Ty Cobb, and is likely to remain his for the foreseeable future. Between 1905 and 1926, Cobb stole home 35 times. Not even Lou Brock is going to come close to surpassing that mark.

★ ★ ★

Jacqueline Hansen, a 27-year-old insurance underwriter from Los Angeles, became the first woman to better the time of 2 hours, 40 minutes in the marathon, when she registered the world record time of 2 hours, 38 minutes, 19 seconds, at Eugene, Oregon, in December, 1975.

★ ★ ★

Marble games date to antiquity and have been common to virtually every civilization. Archaeologists have unearthed marbles from the tombs of Egyptian pharaohs, the prehistoric caves of Europe, and the graves of American Indians. The earliest marbles were fashioned from stone, clay, nuts, and polished wood. Even the knucklebones of sheep were used. Later, marbles were made from marble, agate, porcelain, glass, brass, iron, and steel.

★ ★ ★

Byron Nelson of Fort Worth, Texas, in the period from March 16 to August 15, 1945, won 11 consecutive golf tournaments, a Professional Golfers' Association record. Nelson established another record by winning a total of 19 tournaments that season. His victories included the U.S. Open, the P.G.A., the Canadian Open, and the Canadian P.G.A.

★ ★ ★

In a game between the Detroit Red Wings and the Montreal Canadiens at the Montreal Forum on January 28, 1973, it took Detroit's Harry Boucha only six seconds to score a goal following the face-off that started play. It rates as the fastest opening goal in National Hockey League history.

★ ★ ★

Relief pitcher Mike Marshall of the Los Angeles Dodgers wasn't named the Most Valuable Player in the National League in 1974 (his teammate Steve Garvey won the award), but perhaps he should have been. Marshall appeared in 106 regular-season games that year, an all-time major-league record for a pitcher. He also made appearances in two playoff games, five World Series games, and the All-Star game. In one stretch, Marshall appeared in 13 consecutive games, also a record.

He won 15 of 27 decisions over the regular season, had a 2.42 earned-run-average, and led the National League in games saved with 21. *The Sporting News* named him "Fireman of the Year" and "Pitcher of the Year," and he won the National League's Cy Young Award. The MVP award was the only one he failed to win.

★ ★ ★

In 1922, Ralph Samuelson of Minnesota theorized that skis could support a person in the water pulled by a speeding boat. To produce skis to do the job, he took two pine boards eight feet long and nine inches wide, and curved the tips by steaming them in boiling water. Shortly after, Samuelson became the first water skier on record.

★ ★ ★

In bowling, an open frame is one in which you fail to get either a spare or strike. In the period from May 23 to July 25, 1944, Merrill Weaver of Columbus, Ohio, bowled a record 244 consecutive games in sanctioned league play without a single open frame.

★ ★ ★

George Blanda established pro football's longevity record during the season of 1975, his 26th (and last) in the game. In baseball, Jim McGuire, whose career ended in 1910 when he was wearing the uniform of the Cleveland Indians, played longer than anyone else. Oddly, the record that McGuire holds is exactly the same as Blanda's — 25 seasons.

★ ★ ★

During the racing season of 1919-20, the legendary Man O' War went to the post 21 times, winning all but once. The name of the horse that cost the great champion a perfect record: Upset.

★ ★ ★

In 1976, as a salute to the Bicentennial, the Delaware Sports Club of Wilmington offered a race that was exactly 17.76 kilometers in length (which is equivalent to 11 miles, 70 yards, 1 foot, 2½ inches). Larry Schmelia was the winner, posting a time of 1 hour, 2 seconds, which was, of course, the world record for the distance.

★ ★ ★

Baseball players of the early 1900's often displayed remarkable strength and stamina, at least when compared to players today. One of the most notable of the iron-man performances took place on September 28, 1908, when Big Ed Ruelbach of the Chicago Cubs shut out the Brooklyn Dodgers, 5-0, in the first game of a doubleheader, and then came back in the second game to shut them out again, 3-0.

Golfers rank today as among the highest paid of all athletes, with several earning in excess of two-hundred-thousand dollars annually in prize money alone. But such wasn't always the case. Paul Runyan was golf's leading money winner in 1934, grossing $6,767. His operating expenses that year amounted to $6,765, giving Runyan a net income of exactly $2 for the year.

After a game against the Toronto Metros on July 6, 1975, fans of the Rochester Lancers of the North American Soccer League must have been shaking their heads in wonderment. The Rochester team managed only one shot at the Toronto goal during the game, a record for offensive tranquility that has never been matched.

Pitcher Joan Joyce almost singlehandedly

led the Connecticut Falcons of the International Women's Professional Softball Association to the league championship in 1976, compiling the kind of statistics baseball pitchers only dream about. She earned a 39-2 regular-season record, with a 0.13 earned-run-average. She had four no-hitters and 494 strike outs in 312⅔ innings. She pitched 3-0 and 2-1 victories in the Falcons' four-game sweep of the Western Division champion San Jose, California, Sunbirds in the World Series, and in those two victories, she gave up only four hits and struck out 36.

In major-league baseball, a particularly valuable member of a team is sometimes referred to as "The Franchise." In women's professional softball, Joan Joyce is called "The League."

★ ★ ★

Ted Williams has been called baseball's best hitter of recent times. No one had a better perception of the strike zone. He would not swing at a pitch unless he thought it was within the zone and he thought that he could hit it solidly. Evidence of this is that he led the American League in bases on balls for four consecutive seasons beginning in 1946. And in one stretch beginning on August 24, 1941, he was issued bases on balls in 19 consecutive games, a record no other player has come close to matching.

★ ★ ★

The shortest Olympic champion in history was America's Joseph DePietro, 4-feet, 8 inches in height. A weightlifter in the bantamweight division, DePietro won his gold medal in the 1948 Olympic games in London with a lift of 677.9 pounds.

★ ★ ★

During the 1962 football season, quarterback George Blanda of the Houston Oilers had a record 42 passes intercepted. That statistic gives added luster to a record of Bart Starr's. During 1964, the Green Bay quarterback, known for his pinpoint accuracy, was intercepted only three times.

★ ★ ★

A greyhound named The Shoe established the highest speed record for any dog of that breed when timed a 41.7 miles per hour at Richmond, New South Wales, Australia, on April 25, 1968.

★ ★ ★

Bowling, brought to the United States by early Dutch colonists, mushroomed in popularity in the state of New York and throughout New England during the 1830's and 1840's. People began to bet on games, and gamblers seized upon the sport. Matches involving huge sums were staged, and there were charges of fraud and fixes. As a result, the Connecticut State Legislature passed a law prohibiting "the game of bowling at 9 pins," the standard type of bowling in those days. Bowlers were angered. One individual, whose name has been lost to history, worked out a scheme to circumvent the law, developing a game in which 10 pins were used. A complete set of rules were drawn. The game, called tenpin bowling, flourished, and by the early decades of the 20th century had become popular in almost every part of the United States.

★ ★ ★

The Boston Red Stockings and the Philadelphia Blue Stockings of the National Association became the first baseball teams to travel beyond the continental limits of the United States, when, between July 30, 1874, and August 27, 1874, they toured England and Ireland, playing 15 exhibition games.

★ ★ ★

Only two men have retired undefeated as world heavyweight boxing champions. They are Gene Tunney, who reigned from 1926 to 1928, and Rocky Marciano, the champion from 1952 to 1956.

★ ★ ★

In the years just before he retired in 1975, George Blanda was known chiefly as a field-goal kicker, one of the game's best. But in an earlier day, Blanda had been a quarterback, and kicking the ball was only a sideline. Blanda did the quarterbacking for the Houston Oilers from 1960 through 1966, and he loved to throw the ball. On November 1, 1964, in a game against the Buffalo Bills, he filled the sky with footballs, completing 37 passes on 68 attempts. Both are National Football League records.

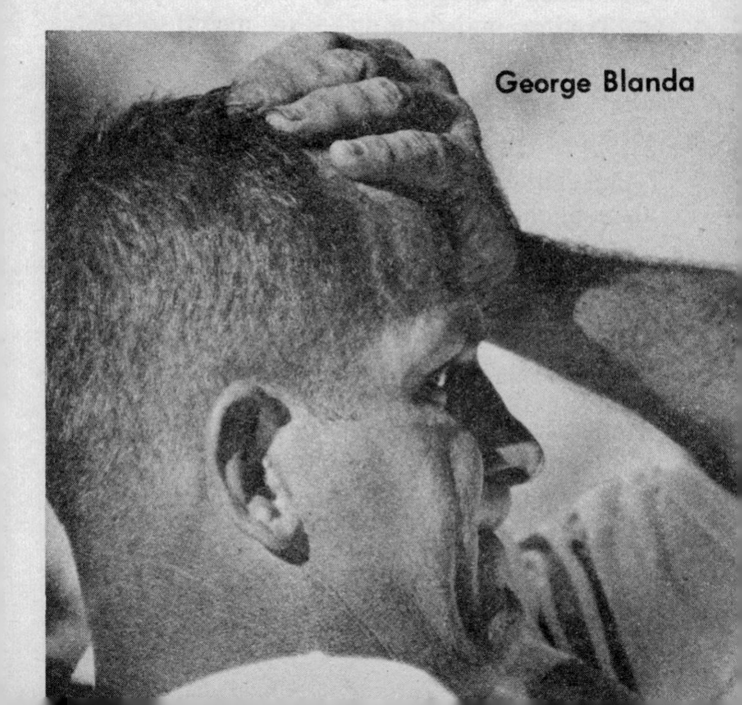
George Blanda

★ ★ ★

The pentathlon, an athletic contest consisting of five events for each competitor, originated in the ancient Olympics and is offered in revised form in the modern Olympics. The event may have been derived from an ancient legend. A muskateer of the king escaped from an enemy dungeon, stole a horse, and set off on a wild dash to safety. When his horse was shot out from under him, he stole a sword and used it to kill one of his pursuers. Then, taking a pistol from the vanquished foe, he battled his way through enemy territory to a wide river beyond which were friendly forces. He swam the river, then ran the rest of the way to safety. The events that make up the pentathlon — horseback riding, fencing, pistol shooting, swimming, and running — are meant to recreate the athletic feats of the muskateer.

★ ★ ★

Baseball banned the spitball in 1920. But the three pitchers in baseball at the time who were "earning their living" with the pitch were allowed to continue using it. One of those three, Burleigh Grimes, who won 270 games in an 18-year career that ended in 1934, was the last pitcher to throw a spitball — legally.

★ ★ ★

College basketball's highest season scoring

average was established in 1954 when Clarence (Bevo) Francis of Rio Grande (Ohio) University averaged 45.5 points per game. Several times that year Francis performed in spectacular fashion, scoring 82 points against Bluffton, 84 against Alliance, and 113 against Hillsdale, the NCAA record for points in a game.

★ ★ ★

As goaltender for the California Seals from 1971-72 through 1974-75, Gilles Meloche never won the Vezina Trophy, never came close, in fact. But in 1974-75 he outdid Ken Dryden, Bernie Parent, Tony Esposito, and all the other more noted goalies of the day when he registered six assists, an all-time National Hockey League record for goalkeepers.

★ ★ ★

During 1977, 18-year-old Julie Shea, competing in the North Carolina girls' high school track championships, won the mile in 4 minutes, 43.1 seconds, a national record. She bettered the previous high school mark by 3.7 seconds.

★ ★ ★

When the Los Angeles Dodgers met the Chicago White Sox on October 6, 1959, at the Los Angeles Coliseum in the fifth game of the

World Series, the largest crowd ever to attend a major league game — 92,706 — watched. But that figure is only a small fraction of the biggest *audience* in baseball history. An estimated 75,900,000 people tuned in on television when the Cincinnati Reds defeated the Boston Red Sox in the seventh game of the 1975 World Series played on Wednesday night, October 22, 1975.

★ ★ ★

When Ethiopian marathoner Abebe Bikila won a gold medal in the 1960 Olympics, he created a sensation, not only by virtue of the fact that he set a record in the event (2 hours, 15 minutes, 16 seconds), but because he ran the 26 miles, 385 yards barefooted. In 1964, Bikila, again barefooted, won the Olympic marathon a second time, becoming the only two-time winner of the event, and he managed to pare his record time by 3 minutes, 5 seconds.

★ ★ ★

The year 1972 was a landmark year for American bicycling enthusiasts. According to the Bicycle Institute of America, it was the first since the 1800's that Americans purchased more bicycles than automobiles.

★ ★ ★

The New York Giants of 1916 compiled a

remarkable winning streak of 26 games, the longest victory string in modern baseball history. Teams usually use such streaks to vault toward the pennant. But the Giants didn't. They finished fourth in the National League standings that season.

★ ★ ★

George Blanda, who played professional football for 26 seasons for four different teams, and ended his playing days in 1975 with the Oakland Raiders, scored a record 2,002 points during his career. He scored nine touchdowns, and booted 335 field goals and 943 extra points. Blanda's record is safe as any record can be. No other player, either active or retired, has scored as many as 1,500 points.

★ ★ ★

The first world heavyweight championship in which boxing gloves were worn and rounds were three minutes in length was between John L. Sullivan and James L. (Jim) Corbett, and took place in New Orleans on September 7, 1892. Corbett won in 21 rounds.

★ ★ ★

America's Ralph Miller set the fastest record claimed for skiing — 109.14 miles an hour — at Portillo, Chile, on August 25, 1955. The average speed of Jean-Claude Killy in winning the

1968 Olympic downhill title was, by comparison, 53.93 miles per hour.

★ ★ ★

Rick Martin's value as a left winger for the Buffalo Sabres of the National Hockey League was signaled in 1971-72, his first season with the team, when he scored 44 goals, most ever for a rookie player.

★ ★ ★

In baseball's early days, the catcher positioned himself 10 or 12 feet behind the batter, and caught the ball on the first bounce. Even so, there were hazards involved, especially on foul tips. Little by little, equipment was developed to protect the catcher. The catcher's mask was invented by Frederick Thayer, captain of Harvard University's baseball team, who obtained a patent for a "face guard or safety mask" on February 12, 1878. The mask was first tried out in a game at Lynn, Massachusetts, on April 12, 1877. James Tyng has been identified as the wearer. The catcher's chest protector made its debut in 1884, and the big mitt that catchers wear debuted in 1891.

Shinguards were first worn by Red Dooin of the Philadelphia Phillies, but the date is uncertain because Dooin sought to conceal the shinguards by wearing them under his stockings. It was considered unmanly to protect oneself with such equipment. Roger Bresnahan, a catcher for the New York Giants in the early 1900's, was the first catcher to have the courage to wear shinguards openly.

★ ★ ★

West Germany's Hans-Werner Grosse established a world record for a glider flight — 907.7 miles — on April 25, 1972.

★ ★ ★

When it comes to bowling perfection, Elvin Mesger of Sullivan, Missouri, stands alone. During his career, Mesger bowled a total of 26 perfect games. Dick Weber of St. Louis and George Billick of Old Forge, Pennsylvania, are tied for second on the list, each with 17 300's.

★ ★ ★

Golfer Johnny Miller established the record for money won in a single season, with earnings totaling $353,021 in 1974.

★ ★ ★

Hank Aaron's remarkable records as a hitter are well known. But few fans are aware that Aaron also holds a record for his ability on the basepaths. Through his long career, Aaron was caught stealing only 72 times. No other player (with 300 or more attempted steals) was caught stealing fewer times than Aaron in all of major-league history.

★ ★ ★

The goalie in ice hockey carries a heavier burden of equipment than any other player in any other sport. His equipment weighs approximately 35 pounds.

★ ★ ★

Larry Mahan of Brooks, Oregon, ranks as the biggest "name" in rodeo riding. Mahan won five consecutive all-around rodeo titles beginning in 1966, tying a record established by Jim Shoulders in 1959. Mahan set the record for prize money in one season in 1969, winning $57,726.

★ ★ ★

Of the active professional bowlers, Earl Anthony of Tacoma, Washington, is the most consistent. His 257.9 bowling average is the highest among touring pros, and helps to explain how he won more tournaments (seven) and more prize money ($111,513) than any other bowler during 1976.

★ ★ ★

At Shea Stadium in New York City on April 22, 1970, pitcher Tom Seaver, then a member of the Mets, blazed a knee-high fastball toward Al Ferrara of the San Diego Padres, the last hitter of the game. When Ferrara swung and missed, he became Seaver's 19th strikeout victim and tenth in a row. Nineteen strikeouts in a game tied a record established by Charles Sweeney of the National League's Providence team in 1884. It has been equaled two other times (by Steve Carlton in 1969, and by Nolan Ryan in 1974). Seaver, however, is the only pitcher to ever record 10 strikeouts in a row.

England's John Lee established the record for walking across the United States from Los Angeles to New York, when, between April 13 and June 6, 1972, he covered the distance in 53 days, 12¼ hours. Barbara Moore set the record for women — 86 days — in 1960.

England's Pedlar Palmer became the youngest boxing champion of all time when he won the bantamweight title in London on November 26, 1895. Palmer was 19 years old. The youngest American champion was Willie Pep, who won the featherweight title in New York on November 22, 1942, his 20th birthday.

Although he was frequently characterized

as a clown, Yogi Berra was a standout catcher in his long career with the New York Yankees. During one period beginning on July 28, 1957, Berra caught 148 consecutive games without making an error, the all-time record.

★ ★ ★

With winning performances in springboard diving and platform diving in both the 1952 and 1956 Olympic Games, Pat McCormick captured four gold medals, more gold medals than any other American woman before or since.

★ ★ ★

Between the years 1936 and 1967, Art Wall, Jr., of Pocono Manor, Pennsylvania, achieved 37 holes-in-one, the highest career total of any professional golfer.

★ ★ ★

Big Ed Delehanty, the best known of five brothers who played major-league baseball, hit .408 in 1899 with the Philadelphia Phillies to win the National League batting championship. Three years later he starred for the Washington Senators and hit .376, good enough to win the American League batting crown. Delehanty is the only player in baseball history to capture the batting championship in both major leagues.

★ ★ ★

Golfer Mary (Mickey) Wright established a course record for a woman professional when she shot a 62 on the Hogan Park Course in Midland, Texas, during November, 1964.

★ ★ ★

Larry Doby, born on December 13, 1924, in Camden, South Carolina, joined the Cleveland Indians in 1947, and carved out a splendid career. He owned a lifetime batting average of .283 when he retired in 1959. But Doby is a notable figure because he was the first black player in the American League. The year that he signed with the Indians was the same year that Jackie Robinson became a Brooklyn Dodger.

★ ★ ★

The all-wood bowling pin has gone the way of football's drop kick and daytime baseball. Pins in use today are made of wood but sheathed in tough plastic. And they are not constructed from a solid wood block, but from a block made of laminated chunks of wood.

The American Bowling Congress sets standards for pins relating to their size, balance, finish, moisture content, and weight. Specifications concerning weight permit the pins to range from 3 pounds, 2 ounces to 3 pounds, 10 ounces, providing the pins on any one set do not vary by more than 4 ounces.

★ ★ ★

Jack Nicklaus established the lowest score in the U.S. Masters in 1965, with an 72-hole total of 271. Nicklaus, with an 18-hole total of 64 that year, tied the record for the lowest round held by Lloyd Mangrum, which Mangrum had set in 1940.

★ ★ ★

The most frequently run distance in the United States is not 100 yards, 100 meters, or even a mile, but 90 feet, the distance between bases in baseball.

★ ★ ★

On August 1, 1975, Willie Callaway, Jr., of Detroit bowled a 298 game, and immediately followed it with a game of 90. According to the American Bowling Congress, the difference in the scores of his two games — 208 pins — was the biggest in bowling history.

★ ★ ★

Playing the Lower Course at the Baltusrol Golf Club in Springfield, New Jersey, during June, 1967, Jack Nicklaus, with a 275, on rounds of 71, 67, 72, and 65, established the lowest

72-hole total in the history of the U.S. Open. Lee Trevino tied the record at the Oak Hill Golf Club at Rochester, New York, in 1968.

★ ★ ★

Billy (Pop) Schriver, a catcher for the Chicago Cubs, acquired some degree of fame in August 29, 1892, when he caught a baseball dropped from the Washington Monument. As if to prove that the catch was no fluke, Schriver performed the stunt again on August 25, 1895.

★ ★ ★

Dick Weber of St. Louis, Missouri, in his almost three decades of championship competition, has won more tournaments, bowled more

Dick Weber

games, knocked down more pins, and won more prize money than any other professional bowler in history. Here is a rundown of Weber's accomplishments (as of January 1, 1977):

Tournaments won: 56
Games: 14,287
Pins: 3,021,756
Earnings: $613,345.90

★ ★ ★

Having good size is as important to being a champion oarsman as it is to playing tackle or guard in football. With each stroke, an oarsman must pull 100 pounds, and there are from 30 to 40 strokes a minute required during a six or eight minute race. The best oarsmen usually weigh 200 pounds or more.

★ ★ ★

While most golfers have never seen a hole-in-one, much less achieved one, they occur with some degree of frequency. On any given day during the peak of the golfing season, as many as a hundred "aces" are likely to be recorded. In 1969, 18,319 holes-in-one were recorded, the most in any calendar year.

★ ★ ★

During the 1970-71 season, the Boston Bruins

established a National Hockey League record by winning 33 games on their home ice. The very next season, as if to prove their versatility, the Bruins set a league record for road victories by winning 26 games in foreign arenas.

★ ★ ★

Cy Young, with 511 victories in his career, won more games than any other major-league pitcher. Young didn't win every time he took the mound, not by any means. He also lost more games than any other pitcher, 315 of them.

★ ★ ★

Beginning with the first of the modern Olympics in 1896, the United States earned a perfect record in the pole vault competition, winning 16 gold medals. The United States was expected to win its 17th gold medal in the event in 1972. Bob Seagren was the nation's leading vaulter at the time. He had won the Olympic gold medal in 1968, and earlier in 1972 he had set a world record, vaulting 18 feet, 5¾ inches. But shortly before competition began, Olympic officials confiscated Seagren's fiberglass poles. Using a borrowed pole, Seagren still managed to finish second. The gold medal went to East Germany's Wolfgang Nordwig, whose winning vault was 18 feet, ½ inch.

★ ★ ★

Ky Michaelson established the speed record for snowmobiling — 114.5 miles per hour — at Mallet's Bay, Vermont, on February 15, 1970.

★ ★ ★

Tommy Moore of Hagerstown, Maryland, playing the 145-yard fourth hole at the Woodbrier Golf Course in Martinsville, West Virginia, on March 8, 1968, became the youngest golfer ever to shoot a hole-in-one. Tommy was barely one month past his sixth birthday at the time.

★ ★ ★

A pitcher's earned-run-average (E.R.A.) is based on an imaginary nine-inning game. To figure an earned-run-average, divide the innings pitched into the earned runs allowed, and then multiply by nine. An earned-run-average of 2.67 indicates that a pitcher has been yielding 2.67 runs for every nine innings he's been pitching. In the season of 1968, Bob Gibson of the St. Louis Cardinals compiled the lowest earned-run-average in major-league history, a remarkable 1.12.

★ ★ ★

Bill A. Johnson of Garden Grove, California, established the official speed record for motorcycles — 224.569 miles per hour — at the Bonneville Salt Flats of Utah on September 5, 1962.

★ ★ ★

During the 1968-69 bowling season, Beverly Ortner of Tucson, Arizona, bowled a three-game series of 818, the highest ever by a woman, according to the official records of the Women's International Bowling Congress.

★ ★ ★

Don Drysdale, who won 209 games in his 14-year career with the Los Angeles Dodgers, was not averse to throwing at a batter if he felt the occasion demanded it. Drysdale was not altogether opposed to hitting a man, either. He led the National League in hit batsmen five times, a record. And when his career ended in 1969, Drysdale held the all-time league record in that department. He had plunked 154 batters.

★ ★ ★

Danny Churchill established the world speed record for water skiing — 125.69 miles per hour — at the Oakland, California, Marine Stadium in 1971.

★ ★ ★

For the worst team in baseball history, you don't have to go back any farther than 1962, the year that the New York Mets, in their first season of operation, won 40 games and lost 120 (a .250 percentage), and finished 60½ games behind the first-place San Francisco Giants.

★ ★ ★

From October 24, 1959, through March 28, 1973, Wilt Chamberlain established himself as one of basketball's most disciplined players. Chamberlain played in a record 1,045 games during that period without once being disqualified because of personal fouls.

★ ★ ★

Russia's Ivan Krumich, a basketball player who stood 7-feet, 3-inches, was the tallest athlete at the 1960 Olympic Games in Rome; he also had the biggest feet. They required size 20 shoes.

★ ★ ★

Stan Mack of New York City, during the period from February 15, 1961, through June 5, 1964, drove a go-kart around the world, beginning and finishing in New York. He covered 23,000 land miles and traveled through 28 countries. Since there is no other known instance of the feat being attempted, Mack is regarded as the world record-holder in the event.

★ ★ ★

Frank Robinson, dismissed as manager of the Cleveland Indians in 1977 after two often turbulent seasons, enjoyed much greater success as a player. In 1961, as an outfielder and third baseman for the Cincinnati Reds, Robinson was voted the National League's Most Valuable Player. In 1966, after being traded to the Baltimore Orioles, he won the balloting as the Most Valuable Player in the American League. Robinson is the only player in baseball history to have won MVP awards in both major leagues.

★ ★ ★

For bowling endurance, no one has been able to match the accomplishment of Bob Atheney of St. Petersburg, Florida, who, beginning on November 9, 1975, rolled 1,976 consecutive games without stopping. The feat required 265 hours. Scarcely three months before, Larry Butler of Sarasota, Florida, rolled a record 1,776 games in a row, but Butler took 309 hours.

★ ★ ★

The summit of Mount Everest, at 29,028 feet,

Frank Robinson

the world's highest mountain, was first reached by Edmund Hillary of New Zealand and Tenzing Norkhay, a Sherpa guide, on May 29, 1953.

★ ★ ★

Baseball playoff series are standard practice today, but it used to be that the first-place team on the last day of the season was deemed the league champion, and went on to participate in the World Series. Baseball's first playoff series took place in October, 1946, and was made necessary when the Brooklyn Dodgers and St. Louis Cardinals ended the season tied. The Cards won the first two of the three games scheduled, and went on to defeat the Boston Red Sox in the World Series.

★ ★ ★

Playing shorthanded, that is, with less than a full complement of players on the ice, is a heavy burden for a hockey team. But playing shorthanded didn't seem to bother the Boston Bruins of 1970-71 very much. They scored a surprising 25 shorthanded goals that season, a National Hockey League record.

★ ★ ★

It's been said that the Gnip Gnop table, introduced in 1977, is going to revolutionize Ping Pong. (Gnip Gnop is Ping Pong spelled backwards.) There's no wood in the Gnip Gnop table. It's made of polyethylene bonded to an aluminum core. Rain, snow, and freezing temperatures have no effect upon it, which could lead to Ping Pong becoming a year-round outdoor activity.

★ ★ ★

The biggest paid attendance in boxing history was recorded when Gene Tunney met Jack Dempsey for the world's heavyweight championship at Sesquicentennial Stadium in Philadelphia on September 23, 1926. A total of 120,757 attended the match.

★ ★ ★

Mexico's Felipe Munoz, winner of a gold medal in the 200-meter breaststroke in the 1968 Olympic Games, might also have been awarded a medal for the most original nickname. Since his mother came from the town of Rio Frio (meaning cold river), and his father was born in Aguascalientes (hot waters), Felipe was dubbed El Tibio (The Lukewarm).

★ ★ ★

Ill fortune helped Payne Rose of St. Louis, Missouri, win a place in the official record manual of the American Bowling Congress.

During a game bowled in September, 1962, Rose suffered six consecutive 7-10 splits.

★ ★ ★

The record books almost always overlook the fact that there were post-season championships in baseball before 1903, the year usually established for the first World Series. Back in 1884, Providence, champions in the National League that year, challenged the New York Metropolitans, the winners in the American Association, to a "championship of the world." (The American League was not in existence at the time; it was not founded until 1901.) The championship series was played at New York's Polo Grounds, and Providence won all three games.

★ ★ ★

Perhaps the most grueling of all sports events is the Iditarod Trail International Championship Sled Dog Race, which covers the 1,049 miles from Anchorage to Nome over some of Alaska's roughest terrain. Competitors must contend with freezing temperatures, fierce winds and storms, and marauding packs of wolves. Jerry Riley of Nenana, Alaska, established a record for the event in 1976, when he and his dogs covered the distance in 18 days, 22 hours, 58 minutes, and 17 seconds.

★ ★ ★

In April, 1976, 16-year-old Eileen Smith of Seaford, New York, the only female entrant in the 68th annual 10-mile walk on the Coney Island boardwalk, won the race in a time of 1 hour, 37 minutes, 12 seconds. She was the first woman ever to win the event.

★ ★ ★

Charles Henry Cooper was pro basketball's first black player. He was drafted by the Boston Celtics on April 24, 1950, and played his first game for the team on November 1 that year against the Fort Wayne Pistons at Fort Wayne, Indiana.

★ ★ ★

Lou Gehrig, although often overshadowed by Babe Ruth during his career with the New York Yankees, did set one record that established him as one of the game's great sluggers. Between 1923 and 1939, Gehrig smashed 23 grand-slam home runs. Hank Aaron, by comparison, had 16 grand slammers.

★ ★ ★

When the Montreal Canadiens faced the Toronto St. Patricks at Montreal on January 10, 1920, no one was prepared for the scoring orgy that took place. A record 21 goals were registered, Montreal winning, 14-7.

★ ★ ★

The greatest number of competitors in any sports event took part in the "Vasa Loop" Nordic skiing race in Sweden on March 4, 1970. There were 9,397 entrants.

★ ★ ★

When Ernie Nevers of the Chicago Cardinals scored six touchdowns against the Chicago Bears in November 28, 1929, he set a record that has been equaled only once (by William [Dub] Jones of the Cleveland Browns in a game against the Chicago Bears on November 25, 1951). But besides his rash of touchdowns against the Bears, Nevers also contributed four points after touchdown, giving him a total of 40 points for the game. And that's a record that no one has equaled.

★ ★ ★

During the 1904 pennant race in the American League, Jack Chesbro of the New York Highlanders went to the mound 53 times, and won 41 games, the modern American League record. But Chesbro did no celebrating. On October 10 that year in a game against the Boston Red Sox, with two out in the ninth inning, Chesbro uncorked a wild pitch, and it cost the New York team the game — and the pennant. One of the most costly mistakes in sports history, the pitch overshadowed Chesbro's stunning victory total for decades.

A skateboarding craze swept the United States during the early 1960's. Then the sport faded, only to be revived during mid-1970's. The revival began when Frank Nasworthy, an engineering student at Virginia Polytechnic Institute, realized that polyurethane wheels, then used on roller skates at roller rinks, could be adapted for skateboard use. Their remarkable traction enabled skateboarders to be much more creative in the tricks they performed. Nasworthy formed a company in 1973 to manufacture boards with polyurethane wheels. They were an instant success. By 1975, 200 skateboard manufacturers were struggling to keep up with the demand.

Professional golfer George Bayer, 6-foot-5, 230 pounds, was the longest driver golf has known. His longest measured drive — 420 yards — was struck at the Las Vegas International in 1953. Playing a 426-yard hole on a Tucson, Arizona, course, Bayer once drove the ball to the flag.

★ ★ ★

Through the season of 1977, the New York Yankees had participated in the World Series 31 times. That's more than the combined appearances of Baltimore, Chicago, Cleveland, Minnesota, Oakland, Boston, Milwaukee, California, Texas, Kansas City, and Seattle.

★ ★ ★

No one ever had to explain the term "home-court advantage" to the Philadelphia 76ers during 1966-67. The team won a record 36 consecutive games that season at Convention Hall, their friendly home.

★ ★ ★

The record for service as a head coach — 57 years — is held by Amos Alonzo Stagg, who coached at Springfield (Massachusetts) College from 1890 to 1891, the University of Chicago from 1892 to 1932, and at the College of the Pacific from 1933 to 1946.

★ ★ ★

Although his name has been all but forgotten, Ray C. Ewry ranks as one of America's outstanding Olympic champions. Ewry, who suffered from rheumatic fever as a child and did not compete until he was 35, won gold medals in the standing high jump and standing broad jump in 1900, 1904, and 1908. He also won gold medals in the standing hop, step, and jump in 1900 and 1904 — a total of eight gold medals. Ewry's medal total was not surpassed until the 1972 Olympic Games, when swimmer Mark Spitz won seven gold medals to go with the two gold medals he had won in the 1968 Olympics.

★ ★ ★

England's A.E. Smith established golf's lowest recorded score at Woolacombe in January 1, 1936, with a 55. The course was 4,248 yards in length. Homero Blancas, an American professional, registered a 55 at the Premier Golf Course in Longview, Texas, on August 19, 1962. The Premier course measured 5,002 yards.

★ ★ ★

Joe McGinnity, who pitched for Baltimore, Brooklyn, and the New York Giants between 1890 and 1908, had an appropriate nickname — "Iron Man." Five times during his career McGinnity pitched both games of a doubleheader, and three times he won both. McGinnity liked to pitch with only two days rest. It didn't seem to do him any harm. During his career, he managed to win 247 games.

★ ★ ★

Volleyball, like basketball, is one of the few "invented" sports. In 1895, William G. Morgan, a student at Springfield College, in Springfield, Massachusetts, and a director of a Y.M.C.A. in nearby Holyoke, experimented with a game in which players struck an inflated rubber ball back and forth across a high net with a hand, fist, or arm. Morgan named the game minonette, but later changed it to volleyball.

★ ★ ★

Ted Lindsay, in a 17-year career with the Detroit Red Wings and Chicago Black Hawks, established himself as the most notorious of hockey's "bad boys." Lindsay compiled a record total of 1,808 penalty minutes, an average of 106 penalty minutes per season.

★ ★ ★

Mickey Mantle of the New York Yankees ranks as baseball's greatest switch hitter of all time. Ten times during his career Mantle hit home runs from both sides of the plate during a game. It's a record that no one else approaches.

★ ★ ★

One well known sport, becoming increasingly popular in the United States, originated by accident. It's rugby.

In 1823, William Ellis, a student at Rugby College in Warwickshire, England, was playing soccer. The rules for soccer were much the same as the rules today — players could only kick the ball — using the hands was prohibited.

But Ellis found the rules a heavy burden, and out of his frustration he picked up the ball, tucked it in his arms, and began running toward the opposition goal. Ellis' breach of the rules embarrassed his teammates, and they apologized to their rivals.

In the days and weeks that followed, Ellis' run was discussed frequently. Some players felt that being able to run with the ball gave added excitement to the game. Experimental contests were held in which running with the ball was allowed.

In 1839, Arthur Pell, a student at Cambridge University, set down rules for a game somewhat similar to soccer, but which permitted running. Ellis' play had always been referred to as "that play at Rugby," and the game that developed was known as "Rugby's game," and, later, simply "rugby."

In the years that followed, the sport spread to schools throughout England. It was being played by students at McGill University in Montreal, Canada, in the 1870's. Rugby competition began in the United States in 1875.

★ ★ ★

Kelso, a thoroughbred foaled in 1957, who raced from 1959 to 1966, won more money than any other horse in history — $1,977,896. In his 63 races, Kelso won 39, came in second 12 times, and was third in two of them.

★ ★ ★

When UCLA defeated Duke in the finals of the NCAA basketball championship in 1964, it began a long period in which the Bruins reigned supreme in college basketball. UCLA captured the title the next year, missed in 1966, but then won the championship seven times in the next eight years. No other team has ever won as many as *three* consecutive championships.

★ ★ ★

For baseball-card collectors, there is no card more highly prized than the one bearing the picture of Honus Wagner. It was issued by Sweet Caporal cigarettes about 1910. Only about a dozen of the cards are still in existence. A single card is valued at well over $1,500.

★ ★ ★

There are more than 60 million bowlers today, rolling for strikes and spares in 47 nations of the world. There's even bowling in the White House, lanes having been installed in the basement for the convenience of the occupants.

Some of baseball's most glittering names have flopped sadly in World Series play. Boston's Ted Williams, in his only World Series appearance, batted only .200 and didn't get one extra-base hit. Bob Feller, the Cleveland ace, waited 10 years to get into a World Series, lost two games, and never got into another one. Brooklyn star Duke Snider batted .143 in his first World Series. Mickey Mantle of the New York Yankees struck out five times and batted .208 in the 1953 World Series.

During 1977, Kathy Rosenberry, a freshman at Golden West College in Newport Beach, California, pitched her team to a record third straight AIAW (Association of Intercollegiate Athletics for Women) softball championship. She finished the season with a 0.55 earned-run-average and did not allow an earned run in 21 tournament innings.

November 6, 1869, is the date usually cited

for the first intercollegiate football game (between Princeton and Rutgers). It took almost another 40 years before uniform numbers for football players were introduced. Players for the University of Pittsburgh were the first to wear them for a game against Washington and Jefferson on December 5, 1908.

★ ★ ★

America's Al (for Alfred) Oerter was an Olympic performer without equal. A discus thrower, Oerter is the only athlete in history to win a gold medal in four consecutive Olympic meets. Not only did Oerter win the discus throw each time, but he established a record with each performance. In 1956, when the games were held in Melbourne, Oerter threw the discus 184 feet, 10 inches. In 1960 at Rome, his throw measured 194 feet, 2 inches. In 1964 at Tokyo, it was 200 feet, 1 inch. And in 1968 at Mexico, 212 feet, 6 inches. No other Olympic athlete in the past half century has managed to earn as many as *three* consecutive gold medals, and the list of two-time winners is a very short one.

★ ★ ★

The longest hole-in-one ever recorded occurred on the 444-yard 10th hole at the Miracle Hills Golf Club, Omaha, Nebraska, on October 7, 1965, on a drive struck by Robert Mitera.

★ ★ ★

During the 1977 baseball season, when home runs began to fly out of baseball parks with startling frequency, there were charges that the baseball had been tampered with, had been enlivened. It had happened many times before, most notably in 1920. Babe Ruth hit 54 home runs that year; the season before he had 29. And in 1918, Ruth had tied Tilly Walker of the Philadelphia A's for the home-run leadership in the American League with a mere 11. Gavvy Cravath of the Philadelphia Phillies won the home-run title in the National League the same year with eight. The lively ball introduced two years later changed all that.

★ ★ ★

Eddie Feigner gained legendary fame as a pitcher in softball. He hurled 530 no-hitters, including 152 perfect games. When giving exhibition performances, Feigner's "team" consisted of only three men besides himself — a catcher, a shortstop, and a first baseman. When Feigner was on the mound, outfielders weren't necessary.

★ ★ ★

Soccer, often hailed as the most popular sport in the world, was once banned by an English king. In 1349, Edward III commanded

England's sheriffs to suppress "such idle practices" as football. The king believed that the game was discouraging interest in archery, upon which the military strength of the country largely depended.

The decathlon, in which each contestant competes in 10 different track and field events, is the most demanding of all Olympic events. When 17-year-old Bob Mathias of Tulare, California, entered the decathlon competition at the 1948 Olympic Games, he had never competed in three of the events — the pole vault, javelin throw, and broad jump. After the first day of competition, Mathias was in third place. On the second and final day, he surged into the lead, compiling a total of 7,139 points. No other competitor surpassed the 7,000-point mark that year. In 1952, Mathias was back again — and won again, becoming the first man in Olympic history to win the grueling decathlon twice.

The longest championship fight under present-day rules took place on September 3, 1906, at Goldfield, Nevada, when Joe Gans of the United States met Denmark's Oscar (Battling) Nelson for the lightweight title. The referee stopped the bout during the 42nd round because of a foul, declaring Gans the winner.

★ ★ ★

Don Meineke, who once played for the National Basketball Association's Fort Wayne Pistons, leads all other players in aggressiveness. During the season of 1967-68, Meineke fouled out of a record 26 games.

★ ★ ★

Yogi Berra's son Dale, who played for a farm team of the Pittsburgh Pirates in 1977, is only one of several young men in baseball whose fathers played in the major leagues. There's also Maury Wills' son Bump, who is a member of the Texas Rangers, and Ken Boyer's son Dave, an infielder in the St. Louis Cardinals' farm system. Hank Sauer's son Henry John is an infielder on a California Angel farm team. Shortstop Eddie Ford, the 23-year-old son of Yankee pitcher Whitey Ford, is owned by the Boston Red Sox. The elder Ford experienced mixed emotions during an exhibition game in the spring of 1977, when his son scored the winning run in a game the Yankees lost.

★ ★ ★

There are two basic lifts in weightlifting: the snatch and the clean and jerk. The snatch requires the weightlifter to pick up the barbell with both hands, in one continuous movement, and hold it over his head motionless. In the clean and jerk, the lifter pulls the weight to his chest, then raises it above his head, arms extended. In the 1976 Olympic Games, super heavyweight L. Plachkov of Bulgaria won the gold medal in the snatch competition, lifting 440.75 pounds. The Soviet Union's V. Alexeev, also a super heavyweight, emerged as the champion in the clean and jerk with a lift of 562 pounds.

On February 7, 1969, Diane Crump became the first woman to ride in a horse race at a major track in the United States. Barbara Jo Rubin became the first woman to ride a winner. On February 22, 1969, she made it to the winner's circle with Cohesian at the Charles Town racetrack in West Virginia.

When Jess Willard fought Frank Morgan at Madison Square Garden in 1916, it resulted in the biggest gate in the Garden's history. A total of $152,000 came through the turnstiles. But the bout was even more noteworthy because it marked the first time that women were permitted to attend a boxing match in the United States.

According to United Press International, the

average salary of baseball regulars in 1977 was $95,149.

★ ★ ★

Arthur Dorrington, who signed with the Atlantic City Seagulls of the Eastern Amateur Hockey League on November 15, 1950, was the first black player in organized hockey. He played for the Seagulls through the 1950 and 1951 seasons.

★ ★ ★

In bowling, a Brooklyn strike is one that smacks into the pins from the left side of the headpin, instead of from the right, which is usual. During the 1975-76 bowling season, Leon Kloeppner of Milford, Connecticut, rolled a perfect game in which every strike was a Brooklyn strike. It was the first Brooklyn 300 ever recorded.

★ ★ ★

Pro-football publicists often cite game attendance figures and television ratings to demonstrate the popularity of their product. Another piece of evidence is the price paid for a one-minute commercial during the telecast of Super Bowl XII in 1978. It cost sponsors a whopping $280,000 per minute to promote their wares, or $4,800 per second.

★ ★ ★

Seventeen-year-old Wayne Grinditch recorded the longest official jump on water skis — 169 feet — at Callaway Gardens, Pine Mountain, Georgia, during July, 1972.

★ ★ ★

The first baseball game at night between major-league teams took place at Crosley Field, Cincinnati, on May 24, 1935, when the Cincinnati Reds defeated the Philadelphia Phillies, 2-1, before a crowd of 20,422. President Franklin Roosevelt participated in the event, pressing a button in Washington that switched on the park's 363 lights mounted on eight huge towers.

★ ★ ★

On June 10, 1977, when skinny, soft-spoken Al Geiberger rolled in a 10-foot putt on the 18th hole in the second round of the $200,000 Danny Thomas-Memphis Golf Classic, he completed the best score ever carded in American professional golf, a 13-under-par 59. The round included 11 birdies and an eagle 3. Geiberger munched on peanut butter and crackers during the course of his round at the Colonial Country Club. The old record of 60 had been set in 1951 by Al Brosch in the third round of the Texas Open at Brackenridge Park Golf Course in San Antonio, Texas, and has been tied six times.

★ ★ ★

The trophy for being the most active — or frantic — bowler of all time goes to Si Hewitt of Lincoln, Nebraska. During the 1968-69 season, Hewitt bowled in a record 17 leagues a week.

★ ★ ★

After Jeff Rice, a 14-year-old sophomore at Allegany High School in Cumberland, Maryland, won the national boys' marbles championship in 1976, he thanked Rick Mawhinney, a former champion, for helping him. "Rick showed me how to shoot with a backspin," said Jeff. "It's really complicated. There's a special way to turn your hand over and squeeze the marble."

In championship contests, 13 marbles are arranged in a cross, or rack, within a circle 10 feet in diameter. The first competitior to knock seven marbles out of the circle with his shooter wins. If the first competitor knocks out seven in a row, it's called a stick, and the game is over. "If you don't use backspin," Jeff Rice says, "your shooter keeps on rolling and goes out of the circle, and you lose your turn. Backspin makes it stop dead, or even roll back."

The national title goes to the winner of a best-of-21 game shootout. Jeff Rice registered a record nine sticks in defeating his opponent. The rules governing marbles do not permit a champion to defend his title, so Jeff's role as a competitor ended the day he captured his national crown.

During the late 1890's, Alvin C. Kraenzlein of the University of Pennsylvania was the track wonder of his day, setting intercollegiate, national, and world records in several sports. Still, no one was prepared for what he accomplished in the Olympic Games in Paris in 1900. Pitted against the best performers in the world, Kraenzlein won the 60-meter sprint, the 110-meter high hurdles, the 200-meter low hurdles, and the running broad jump. Not only did he win four events, something never achieved before, but he set an Olympic record in each.

David Thompson, forward for the Denver Nuggets of the National Basketball Association, is known for his exceptional jumping ability. From a standing start, Thompson can leap straight up 42 inches. This means that the soles of his sneakers are 3½ feet in the air, and the top of his head (Thompson stands 6-foot-4) is within two inches of the rim.

In baseball, when the term "perfect game" is mentioned, the name Don Larsen immediately comes to mind. Pitching for the New York Yankees against the Brooklyn Dodgers in the fifth game of the 1956 World Series, Larsen faced only 27 batters in a no-hit, no-run performance. The feat has been accomplished three times since — by Jim Bunning of the Phillies of June 21, 1964; by Sandy Koufax of the Dodgers on September 9, 1965; and Jim (Catfish) Hunter of the A's on May 8, 1968.

There has been one other perfect-pitching performance, and it is perhaps more masterful than any of the others. On the night of May 26, 1959, Harvey Haddix of the Pittsburgh Pirates pitched 12 perfect innings against the Milwaukee Braves, retiring 36 batters in a row, an unprecedented achievement. But Haddix wound up as the losing pitcher. His teammates were unable to score a run for him, and in the 13th inning Joe Adcock of the Braves got his team's first hit, sending home Felix Mantilla who had reached first base on an error. Thus, one of baseball's most superlative performances turned out to be a losing effort.

★ ★ ★

Women seldom outdo men in track and field events, but there are exceptions. One of the most notable in recent years took place in 1975 in the annual Midnight Sun Marathon in Fairbanks, Alaska. Twenty-one-year-old Marian May set a course record of 3 hours, 2 minutes, and 41 seconds, while defeating 52 rivals, most of them men.

★ ★ ★

The poodle is the most popular dog in the United States according to registration figures of the American Kennel Club, and has ranked as America's favorite since 1950. However, dogs trained to guard property are beginning to crowd the poodle in terms of popularity. German shepherds are No. 2 on the American Kennel Club's list, and Doberman pinschers are fourth. Also in favor are such larger breeds as Irish setters, Labradors, golden retrievers, English sheep dogs, Siberian huskies, and Saint Bernards.

★ ★ ★

When Sugar Ray Robinson won the world middleweight championship by beating Carmen Basilio at Chicago Stadium on March 25, 1958, he became the only boxer in history to win a world title five times. Robinson's other victories were over Jake LaMotta on February 14, 1951; Randy Turpin on September 12, 1951; Carl (Bobo) Olson on December 9, 1955; and Gene Fullmer on May 1, 1957.

★ ★ ★

Italy's Giuseppe Cantarella established the world's speed record for roller skating — 25.78 miles per hour — at Cantania, Italy, on September 28, 1963.

★ ★ ★

In the period from 1956 to 1960, Johnny Unitas of the Baltimore Colts threw touchdown passes in 47 consecutive games. It's a record that Unitas is certain to keep for years to come. Daryle Lamonica, the onetime Oakland Raiders' quarterback, is the No. 2 man on the list. Lamonica tossed touchdown passes in a mere 25 consecutive games.

★ ★ ★

Bowlers often wonder whether it's possible to convert the horrendous 7-10 split. It is possible — but it's highly improbable. During one recent year, the American Bowling Congress reported that 7-10 splits had been converted into spares 2,831 times. That may seem like a sizeable number, but it's not when you consider that a billion or so games were bowled that year.

These statistics make the feat of converting *two* 7-10 splits in one game seem incredible, yet it's been done five times, according to the ABC, most recently in 1966 by Vaughn Lemmond of Daytona Beach, Florida.

★ ★ ★

Baseball's longest game lasted 26 innings. The record in softball is 42 innings. The game was played in 1942 at Kenosha, Wisconsin, and was won by the Italian-American Club. Its

Johnny Unitas

pitcher, Corky Vorraeini, went the distance, winning, 1-0.

★ ★ ★

The dimples on a golf ball are not mere decoration. They have a purpose. Each creates a tiny area of turbulence as the ball surges through the air, causing aerodynamic lift. The ball travels farther as a result.

★ ★ ★

When, in 1975, Topps Chewing Gum sponsored its first bubble-gum blowing contest among major-league baseball players, the results were embarrassing for the company. The winner was Kurt Bevacqua of the Milwaukee Brewers. Topps officials, in reviewing Bevacqua's unimpressive record for the previous season, had decided that he would not be a major-league player in 1975, and had never issued a card with his picture on it.

★ ★ ★

The Big Ten Conference used to be the biggest supplier of talent for the National Basketball Association. But in recent years the Big Ten has been supplanted by the Pacific 8. During the 1976-77 season, 28 NBA players were from Pac-8 colleges. UCLA was the leading college, with 12 players on NBA teams.

★ ★ ★

Skater Sonja Henie ranks as one of the most exceptional figures to grace the world of sports. In 1924, at the age of 10, she won her first title, the figure-skating championship of Norway. She then went on to win one title after another, including:

• Norwegian Championship (6) — 1924, 1925, 1926, 1927, 1928, 1929.

• European Championship (8) — 1929, 1930, 1931, 1932, 1933, 1934, 1935, 1936.

• World Championship (10) — 1927, 1928, 1929, 1930, 1931, 1932, 1933, 1934, 1935, 1936.

• Olympic Championship (3) — 1928, 1932, 1936.

At the close of the 1936 Olympics, Miss Henie abandoned amateur skating to become a professional, journeying to the United States to star in her own ice shows and 11 motion pictures. Millions of Americans flocked to see her over the next two decades. Sonja Henie died in 1969. During her lifetime she amassed a fortune of $47,500,000. No other sports figure, from a financial standpoint, at least, has been as successful.

★ ★ ★

In bowling parlance, a triplicate is a three game series in which the scores for all three games are the same. On March 21, 1965, Jim

Schroeder of Ottawa, Ohio, bowled three consecutive games of 279, the highest triplicate of all time.

★ ★ ★

The world record for a quarter horse over the quarter-mile distance is 21.02 seconds. That's an average speed of 46.48 miles per hour, making the quarter horse the fastest accelerating horse in the world.

★ ★ ★

Some pitchers seem to have a "jinx" over one particular club, and are almost assured of defeating that team simply by showing up at the ball park. For example, the Giants' Christy Mathewson, in the period from June 16, 1904 to September 15, 1908, beat the St. Louis Cardinals 24 consecutive times.

But it sometimes works the other way: a team gets a hex on a particular pitcher. In a stretch from April 23, 1966 to July 24, 1969, the Dodgers' Don Sutton lost to the Chicago Cubs 13 straight times.

★ ★ ★

Most fans of the Chicago Bears are aware that George Halas, the founder of the team and its chairman of the board, once played end for the team. What many fans don't realize is that Halas also once wore the pinstripes of the New

York Yankees. An outfielder, he played 12 games for the Yanks in 1919, batting .091.

★ ★ ★

John Pezzin of Toledo, Ohio, established bowling's official record for consecutive strikes when on March 4, 1976, Pezzin rolled 33 strikes in a row. In his three-game series, Pezzin got nine strikes in the first game, and then bowled two consecutive 300 games.

★ ★ ★

The Stanley Cup, symbol of ice-hockey supremacy, is the oldest professional trophy in America. It was first won in 1894 by the Montreal Amateur Athletic Association. The trophy came into the possession of the National Hockey League in 1917, and has since become emblematic of the world's professional championship. The Montreal Canadiens have won the Stanley Cup more frequently than any other team. In the 26 years between 1952 and 1978, the Canadiens took the Cup home 15 times.

★ ★ ★

Ron Hunt, who played for five different major league teams in a 12-year career that began in 1963, holds a major-league record that no one is trying to break. Hunt was hit by pitches 243 times. In one season, 1971, Hunt was hit 50 times (also a record), or on an average of about once every three games. "I crowd the plate. I don't give away any ground," Hunt once said. How did he feel about his record? "It's not something you brag about," he said.

★ ★ ★

Sixteen-year-old Chuck Linster of Wilmette, Illinois, with 6,006 consecutive push-ups in 3 hours, 54 minutes, on October 5, 1965, established the world record for the exercise.

★ ★ ★

During the 1976-77 season, the Cleveland Cavaliers could boast the biggest team in pro basketball. The average Cavalier stood 6-foot-7 and weighed 211 pounds.

★ ★ ★

When baseball players discuss hitting and hitters, they talk in terms of averages. In the case of base stealing, the number of bases stolen is what is important. But what if base stealing records were based on averages, with players being rated on the basis of the highest percentage of successful steals? Who would be the standout player: Perhaps it would be Bobby Bonds of the Texas Rangers. In the period between 1968 and 1974, Bonds was successful in 263 of 326 attempted steals, an .807 average, an all-time record.

★ ★ ★

The shortest fight on record took place at Palmerton, New Zealand, on July 8, 1952. Ross Cleverly decked D. Emerson with his very first punch. When the referee stopped the bout, a total of seven seconds had elapsed.

★ ★ ★

When the Washington Redskins played the New York Giants on November 27, 1966, the defensive teams took the afternoon off. One touchdown piled upon another, and more points were scored (113) than any other game in pro-football history, the Redskins winning, 72-41. A total of 16 touchdowns were recorded, 10 by the Redskins, six by the Giants.

★ ★ ★

On June 30, 1899, Charles C. Murphy mounted his bicycle to attempt a world-speed record over a wooden track laid down between the rails of the Long Island Railroad near the town of Hempstead. A railroad car was to pace Murphy over a measured mile course. By the time the measured strip was reached, the train was traveling at 60 miles an hour. Murphy kept pace; he did better, in fact. He sped over the mile distance in a record 57 4/5 seconds, becoming the first cyclist to demonstrate that a human could pedal a bicycle at a speed in excess of a mile a minute.

★ ★ ★

The Phillies' Robin Roberts, who led the National League in victories four times while compiling 286 wins for his career, didn't like to throw at batters in an effort to keep them off balance. He was afraid he'd seriously injure someone. Roberts' niceness proved costly, however. No one ever hesitated about digging in when he was on the mound. During one season, 1956, Roberts yielded a record 46 home runs, and he gave up 502 home runs during his career, another record.

★ ★ ★

Cheryl Stearns, a 20-year-old parachutist from Scottsdale, Arizona, captured first place in the women's division of the 1976 U.S. National Parachuting Championships held in Tahlequah, Oklahoma, and set a world record for accuracy among women by scoring 19 consecutive dead-center landings.

★ ★ ★

When the World Cup soccer championship was held in Mexico in 1970 (with Brazil winning), a television audience estimated at one billion — one out of every three of the world's inhabitants — watched with either the "live" transmission of the event or a taped replay.

★ ★ ★

Competing in the second round of the U.S. Open championship at Cherry Hills Country Club, Denver, Colorado, on June 10, 1938, Ray Ainsley took 19 strokes on the par 4 16th hole, a tournament record. Most of the strokes were taken in an effort to get the ball out of a brook.

★ ★ ★

During the period of 1903 through 1952, baseball's two major leagues were made up of the same eight teams representing the same eight cities. No new teams were ever added; none were switched. After the Boston Braves moved to Milwaukee in 1953, teams began to jump around, and when the 1978 season opened, baseball offered 12 teams in the National League and 14 in the American League. Of those 26 teams, only 10 were original clubs that had never been moved. They were: the Boston Red Sox, Cleveland Indians, Chicago Cubs, Chicago White Sox, Cincinnati Reds, Detroit Tigers, New York Yankees, Philadelphia Phillies, Pittsburgh Pirates, and St. Louis Cardinals.

★ ★ ★

In Johnstown, Pennsylvania, on October 28, 1952, Southmont High School defeated Dale

High School in football, 33-27, without making a single first down.

After New Zealand's Peter Snell won the 800-meter race in the 1960 Olympic Games and was awarded his gold medal, he lodged a formal protest, complaining that the medal was not solid gold as he had expected it would be, but merely gold plated. Officials explained to Snell that while medals of solid gold had been distributed in the early Olympic Games, the practice had been discontinued in 1932. Snell's disappointment did not prevent him from entering the 1964 Olympics. He won again at the distance of 800 meters, and he also captured the 1,500-meter event. He accepted both gold medals without complaint.

Tennis star Billie Jean King, often ranked as the most famous female athlete in sports history, was named Woman Athlete of the Year by the Associated Press in 1967 and again in 1973. She is the only woman to have won the award twice.

Paddy Driscoll of the Chicago Cardinals won a place in the National Football League's official record manual when he booted four field goals in a game against the Columbus Tigers in October 11, 1925. Dozens of players have kicked more field goals in a game than Driscoll did — the record is seven — but Driscoll's made the record book because of the *kind* of kicks they were. All were dropkicks.

The technique of dropping the ball and kicking it as it rebounded was as prevalent in the early 1920's as place-kicking is today. The football was rounder in those days, resembling a rugby ball. But when the football began to develop pointy ends, the era of the dropkick began to fade. It was difficult to get a true bounce with the pointed-end ball.

Some coaches feel the dropkick has many advantages and could be useful today. It gives the kicking team another blocker (since no one is needed to hold the ball), and it enables the kicker to get the ball higher in the air, cutting down on blocked kicks. But don't expect to see dropkicks become popular overnight. There's scarcely a coach in football who knows how to teach the art.

★ ★ ★

The longest canoe journey in history was made by Geoffrey Pope and Sheldon Taylor from New York City to Nome, Alaska, a distance of 6,000 miles. The trip, begun on April 25, 1936, took 1 year, 3 months, and 17 days.

★ ★ ★

A passed ball is a baseball pitch missed by the catcher that allows a base runner to advance. Bill Dickey of the New York Yankees did not permit a single passed ball during the season of 1931, and Dickey caught 130 games that year. Compare that with a record established by Charles Hines of the Boston Braves in 1881. In 60 games, Hines allowed 99 passed balls, an average of one to two a game. Why the enormous difference? In Hines' day the catcher was not equipped with a big mitt, but wore only small padded gloves (on both hands), similar to the gloves that batters wear today. So catching the ball, or even managing to stop it, was no easy matter.

★ ★ ★

Like baseball, football, and other professional sports, bullfighting has produced its superstars. The first was Manolete, often ranked as the greatest bullfighter of all time. His full name was Manual Rodriquez Sanchez. Absolutely fearless, a master swordsman, Manolete dominated bullfighting for a dozen years until 1947, the year he was fatally gored.

From the mid 1960's to the early 1970's, El Cordobes — Manual Benitez — was the reigning king of bullfighting. His flamboyant and unorthodox style earned him wide acclaim in Spain and throughout Latin America, although purists often scorned him. El Cordobes retired from the bullring in 1971.

★ ★ ★

Only once in National Hockey League history has a team allowed an average of less than one goal per game. It happened in the 1928-29 season when the Montreal Canadiens permitted only 43 goals in 44 games, an average of .98 goals per game.

★ ★ ★

Baseball umpires and pro basketball and hockey referees are employeees of their respective leagues. The game is their profession. Not in pro football. Take, for example, Super Bowl XI, played in January 1977. Referee Jim Tunney was the assistant superintendent of schools in Bellflower, California. Umpire Lou Palazzi was a landscape architect in Scranton, Pennsylvania. Head linesman Ed Marion worked as an insurance man in Portland, Maine. Line judge Bill Swanson was a bank vice-president in Libertyville, Illinois. Back judge Tom Kelleher was an executive with a plastics company in Philadelphia, and field judge Armen Terzian was a San Francisco school teacher.

★ ★ ★

Those who argue that Ty Cobb was the greatest hitter in baseball history have no trouble supporting their claim. Many of Cobb's accomplishments make those of modern day hitters seem pale by comparison. Among the records Cobb holds are the following:

- Highest lifetime batting average: .367
- Most seasons with batting average of .300 or higher: 23
- Most seasons leading the major leagues in batting: 11
- Most seasons leading his league in batting: 12

★ ★ ★

Australia's Dawn Fraser was a competitive swimmer with few equals. In Olympic competition, she won the 100-meter freestyle in 1956, 1960, and 1964, setting an Olympic record for the event each time. Her winning time in 1964 — 59.5 seconds — remained a record until 1972. She won a fourth gold medal as a member of Australia's 100-meter freestyle relay team in 1956.

★ ★ ★

The oldest tennis court in the world is located in Paris. It was built in 1496.

★ ★ ★

Boccie (BOTCH-ee), played in Italy and Italian communities in the United States, is one of the oldest of all bowling games. The standard playing area, enclosed with boarded ends and sides, is from 78 to 92 feet in length, and from 13 to 19½ feet in width. The surface is covered with hard-packed sandy soil.

Each player takes his turn in rolling or throwing a wooden ball, slightly larger than a baseball, toward a smaller wooden ball, called a "jack." The idea is to bring the ball as close as possible to the jack. Players — four to a side — can use the sideboards in placing their throws. More than 2,000 years ago, when the Caesers ruled what is now Italy, boccie was played there, and the game has changed little through the centuries.

The longest boxing bout in history took place on April 6, and 7, 1893, and lasted 110 rounds, or 7 hours, 19 minutes. Andy Bowen and Jack Burke were the opposing fighters. New Orleans was the scene. When neither man answered the bell for the 111th round, the referee declared it "no contest."

Jackson Haines was a struggling teacher of ballet at the time of the outbreak of the Civil War. In 1863, as his business continued to decline, Haines went to Austria, knowing that ballet was more popular there.

While in Austria, Haines became interested in ice skating. He noticed that skaters moved about aimlessly on the ice. Haines got the idea of teaching ballet movements to skaters, and began showing them how to glide, twist, and spiral. This new form of skating — called fancy skating then, and figure skating today — became popular throughout Europe, and was later introduced to the United States and Canada.

Haines also performed novelty acts on the ice, including the feat of walking on stilts. He established skating schools in Austria and many other European countries. When he died in Finland in 1875, a monument was erected in his honor that proclaimed him the "American Skating King."

★ ★ ★

Kicker Tommy Davis joined the San Francisco 49ers in 1959, and remained with the team for six years. During that time, he established himself as one of the most consistent kickers the game has known. He attempted 350 points after touchdown and missed only two, for an amazing 99.4 percentage. During one stretch, Davis booted a record 234 consecutive points after touchdown.

★ ★ ★

On the afternoon of June 10, 1892, Wilbert Robinson, a catcher for the Baltimore Orioles, came to bat seven times in a game against St. Louis, and hit safely each time, rapping out six singles and a double. Robinson's seven-for-seven performance seems unbeatable. Indeed, no one even matched the feat for more than three-quarters of a century, or until September 16, 1975, when the Pirates' Rennie Stennett lashed out seven hits in a game.

After Russia's Olga Korbut won gold medals on the balance beam and for her floor-exercise routine in the 1972 Olympic Games, enchanting the spectators with her smiles and hand waves, she reigned as the most popular figure in the history of sports in the Soviet Union, displacing the nation's previous favorites, the

Olga Korbut

chess masters. Olga added to her popularity with a triumphant tour of the United States in 1973. She became so well known that letters sent to her from young American fans, and addressed simply, "OLGA, MOSCOW," were delivered without difficulty.

★ ★ ★

Baseball managers today are usually very quick to use relief pitchers, yanking the starting man at the first sign he's tiring. That's why a record set by the great Cy Young is in no jeopardy. Between the years 1890 and 1911, Young started in 818 games and completed 751 of them.

★ ★ ★